THE
ILIAD
OF
HOMER

THE ILIAD OF HOMER

Shortened and in a New Translation
By I. A. RICHARDS

W · W · NORTON & COMPANY

New York · London

First published as a Norton paperback 1958; reissued 1993

W. W. Norton & Company, Inc.
500 Fifth Avenue, New York, N.Y. 10110
W. W. Norton & Company Ltd.
10 Coptic Street, London WC1A 1PU

ISBN 0-393-00101-6

PRINTED IN THE UNITED STATES OF AMERICA

8 9

INTRODUCTION

THE STATISTICAL nature of *messages* is entirely determined by
the character of the source. But the statistical character of the
signal is actually transmitted by a channel . . . is determined
both by what one attempts to feed into the channel and by the
capabilities of the channel to handle different signal situations.
. . . Error and confusion arise and fidelity decreases, when, no
matter how good the coding, one tries to crowd too much over
a channel.

WARREN WEAVER, *Recent Contributions
to the Mathematical Theory of Communication*

THE STYLE of this version has been shaped by
many aims. I hope and believe that they have
settled their worst differences behind the scenes.
But no one who has ever thought about the trans-
lation of remote texts can suppose that there is an ideal ver-
sion for any *general* purpose. My compromise has at least
tried to be conscious, to know what it is giving up for what,
and to accept consistently its own limitations. A brief ac-
count of these "behind the scenes" deliberations will be the
best way to explain how this version differs from others and
why it should have been made.

Let me say first, if I can, what I take to be the chief *general* interest of the *Iliad* for present-day readers. I stress the word "general" not only because the *Iliad* has a place in so many programs of General Education, and because work in one such program first made me feel a need for some version of this kind, but because specialized scholarship today rarely has any direct concern with the general reader. Its own business has become too exacting. And the scholar today tends to forget what the unprepared reader most needs and is apt to offer some introductory steps to scholarship in its place. The general reader's first need is to see for himself why and how the *Iliad* should matter at all to him in these days. Contemporary opinions about the highly conjectural facts of its origin and circumstances do not, I think, help us to see this. Nor need we expect that better opinions still would be more helpful. After all, until only the other day most readers have been without any reputable views whatsoever on such points.

The chief general interest of the *Iliad* is that we can find in it the ancestors to very important things which are still characteristic of European or "Western" culture. Among these are tragedy; the problem character; domestic comedy; an ironic skepticism as to divine concern with or control of human endeavor; certain admirations for the individual will in its pride, and for the heroic conflict that elicits this pride; and, over all, a poetic enjoyment of the foreknowledge of death. "Whence cometh wisdom? and where is the place of understanding?" asks the Book of Job: "Destruction and Death say, 'We have heard a rumor thereof with our ears.'" (28:22) The *Iliad* is the place where that rumor sounds most insistently and with least competition from messages purporting to be more certain. It is a rumor to which modern ears are certainly being tuned.

An anthropology we can as yet only dream of would be needed to say whether these things are really as peculiar to and distinctive of European culture as they seem (or where the limits to this construct, "European culture," should be set). But certainly in our tradition, the *Iliad* is the primal appearance of them—an appearance so clear and so heightened by the strangeness of the setting that it is actually easier to discern and meditate upon these traits in the *Iliad* than in the more complex and cross-bred lineaments of its cultural descendants. The great figures of the *Iliad* are very obviously more than life size. They resemble the glass flowers of the celebrated Harvard collection in being easier to comprehend than any field specimens we may pick for ourselves. And it is not only their physical aspects that are exaggerated: the power to lift a stone, "one that two men could not lift as men are." Their scale in every aspect is magnified as much as Ares and Athene are on Achilles' shield (18), "the people at their feet are smaller"—among whom we may count ourselves along with all other actual persons. Most evidently, certain of their passions are enlarged. Achilles' wrath and his sorrow strike us as exorbitant; our own tracks are not as his. And the momentum of these passions is as remarkable; nothing can halt or divert his anger against Agamemnon except a still greater anger against Hector (and himself) which channels it off. This second rage is so extreme that in the end it offends even the gods, and illustrates once for all the etymologic sense of *wroth* as "crooked, bad." Behind both the anger and the sorrow (in its early phases, at least) is an exclusive self-regard and an oblivion of others which socialized consciences find hard to conceive. A modern nationalist is apt to think that such nonparticipation in the war effort deserves a court-martial and a death penalty. It may help us to compare Achilles not with an individual but with a nation; we may then find that the behavior of most great powers is still only too Achillean. This vanity, this tenderness for our honor, which we no longer dare nurse for ourselves, we can still indulge when we have transferred it to our cause or to our country.

For good or for evil these traits have been essential parts of the spiritual physiognomy of the West. We must consider each for himself whether they are components of an elixir or of a poison. It is idle to ask how far Homer, directly and indirectly, has been responsible for their continuance. We do not know enough about spiritual genetics to say. The point rather is that in the *Iliad* we can study these things in a peculiar purity. The very fact that the setting is strange and remote to us, that the concomitants are often unintelligible or conjectural only, throws what we share with Hector or Helen or even with Hera into relief. When all else differs, what is in common stands out most clearly. And no one can say that what he recognizes in the *Iliad* is not his own deep concern.

I have commented upon the pride and sense of honor, the rage and the grief of Achilles. More easily recognizable, perhaps, is the enigma he is to himself and to all about him, even

to Thetis, his own goddess mother. She takes, indeed, at
times a relatively simple view of him, as mothers sometimes
do. What is troubling him, she thinks, is the loss of his girl,
Briseis; and Achilles himself in Book 9 talks for a moment
as if this were almost so. It is customary to say that the
Iliad is not a love story. I have begun to encourage doubts
and I have given salience in my version to anything that
could support them. It is not much. What is certain is that
Achilles does not know himself. Nonetheless he is the first
character in literature who has definitely embarked on the
endless venture of self-knowledge. He is as truly a problem
character as Hamlet. It would be going too far, no doubt, to
call him a psychological study. But those who like to play
with such things can find food for speculation. There is his
mother, so unwillingly the wife of a mortal, with a twofold
life which is reflected in her son's twofold fate. There is that
questionable character, Phoenix, and the account he gives of
the spoiling of a brat. Being accursed and sonless himself, he
has had very personal ends in view in his education of
Achilles. Patroclus, too, came to Peleus' court under odd cir-
cumstances. Kindhearted though he is, he is not exactly a
timid person—but he behaves as though Achilles were an
A-bomb on a hair-trigger. And rightly. In the great final
scene, when he has yielded to Priam's prayer, Achilles is still
so unsure of himself that he keeps Hector's body out of
Priam's sight. He is afraid that a cry from Priam might yet
unloose his own murderous hands.

The other character in the *Iliad* as mysterious as Achilles
is Helen. She, too, is incomprehensible to herself but with a

continuing depth of self-blame impossible to Achilles. The rest of the mortals, distinct though each one of them is, are wholly at home with themselves. We may think that the women perhaps more resemble our contemporaries than the men.

Above them in one sense, far below them in another, are the gods and goddesses. In spite of the handicap of immortality, and the ironic obliquities, the immortals are still personalities, true to themselves if to nothing else, and fully rounded. A remarkably definite family group is thus projected into heaven. That is a suggestive place for the first appearance of the parental "scene" and interesting evidence for the influence of the family constellation. It is as though the poet, or the poetic tradition, could find no better image for the governance of events than in memories of household dissensions a highly detached and observant child had witnessed. But this, I think, overlooks the humor of these depictions and their "judicious levity." Their lack of bitterness is as surprising as their freedom from speculation or conviction. There are, of course, innumerable questions of a theologic order which these domestic dramas may raise in later minds. But there is really no theology upon Olympus, not a bit more than on Ida in Book 14. There is not even any religion, in strong contrast to the deep religion in the prayers and offerings of the mortals. The malice and jealousy, the trickeries and whims, the disguises, deceits, and treacheries of the immortals raise no moral problems, except to those who remove them from the plot of the *Iliad* and put them into other contexts. Plato did that and condemned them—

to the great and permanent advantage of theology. He was being very unjust to Homer, and finding blasphemy where there was perhaps not even religion. "The monkeyshines of the Olympians" form a comic screen hiding the unthinkable Fate that waits even for them—a screen against which whatever might seem futile in the brief dance of the mortals can gain its due dignity and its pitiful grandeur, undwarfed by astronomic unsearchables.

A version that will let us consider these things as undistractedly as we may must give up some other aims. Among them will be the attempt to reflect the *language* of the *Iliad:* its archaism; its decorative stylized figuredness; its artificiality, and most of its characteristics as a medium for oral extempore composition. A very large proportion of the *Iliad* consists of line-beginnings, lines, and line-endings which the poet could use very freely over and over again, knowing them to be metrically satisfying and sufficiently neutral as regards the context of what he was saying to raise no difficulties for him or for his audience. Most of the stock epithets annexed to the characters, the formal openings and transitions, and many of the similes and descriptive fillings are essentially ready-made *rests,* for the poet and his hearers, by which the strain of composition, and of comprehension for the listeners, can be lessened. They are, of course, by no means inert matter or mere scaffolding; but they have, as it were, a general not a specific duty. They are cells of the poetry that have been found, through generations of experience in public recitation, to serve best as connective tissue, supporting without hindering the more important cells in which the main work of the poem is being forwarded. In a prose version, addressed primarily to a reader's eye, not to a listener's ear, most, though not all, of the necessities of oral epic are best omitted. In print they do not have effects at all like their effects in a flow of metrical utterance.

On the other hand the reign of writing looks like drawing soon to a close. The radio may be restoring to the ear some of its original priority in "literature." The very fact that the highest achievements of verbal communication have to be named with a word which implies letters is evidence of the deep change that the invention of writing made. Between the age of Homer, whenever that was, and Plato's time, were born the concept and the abstraction, as the literate have known them since. And it is this shift from concrete, image-borne, continuous presentations to the products of analysis, comparison, and definition which chiefly comes between a present-day reader and the preintellectual world of Homer. It is impossible to doubt that writing was a prime agent in this change. The eye can linger over individual words and phrases. It can isolate them for reflection. Writing indeed can separate them as they can hardly be separated in preliterate speech. It can give them a distinct and questionable standing, and expose them to a discussion which purely oral-aural communication barely permits. When we stop to consider what is being said, we are probably using powers of controlled, selective attention which we owe to experience with writing. A chief difficulty in rendering the *Iliad* is to remember that it is not concerned with ideas as we have come to understand ideas. Its meanings are more rounded, self-supporting, and whole. Without being any less selective in their own way they are not discriminated and prepared for logical manipulation. Thus the attempt to say with modern English what the *Iliad* says in preliterate speech must reckon with a radical change in *saying* itself. It is not only that different things are said, and said in different ways, but what is done in and by the saying is different.

One resource in this predicament is to return to the condition of the listener, and one motive behind this version has been to make something which can be read aloud without discomfort and grasped by a listener without overfrequent lapses of attention. Its germ, in fact, was a presentation of "The Anger of Achilles" in eight fifteen-minute readings for the Lowell Institute Co-operative Broadcasting Council. From classroom efforts, I knew that available prose versions would not do. No reader, without feeling unbearably stuffy, can mouth any long sequence of such sentences as: "Strange goddess, why art thou minded to beguile me thus? Verily thou wilt lead me yet further on to one of the well-peopled cities of Phrygia or lovely Maeonia, if there, too, there be some one of mortal men who is dear to thee, seeing that now Menelaus hath conquered goodly Alexander, and is minded to lead hateful me to his home. It is for this cause that thou art now come hither with guileful thought." Helen vanishes completely behind such a veil of disused forms. The listener might gather she talked some sort of antique and never actual lingo, but not that he would miss anything by switching to another station. A much simpler and more natural language was clearly needed.

I am anxious not to be unfair to these elaborate attempts to reflect the actual language of the *Iliad*. They serve the highly important purpose of helping people to observe the peculiarities of the Greek. And a scholar with the Greek in his mind no doubt in time becomes almost unaware of the artificial, un-English character of his painfully contrived simulacrum. And Greekless readers, too, may in time grow inured to its strangeness and even become attached to it through familiarity. "Bethink thee now of impetuous valor!" Though no one can imagine anyone ever saying it in any living language, this does somehow tell us what it means. And it is not flat. It is inspiriting and breathes out an air of enterprise. Indeed in concocting my own version, I do not know how often I have found it useful to address my despondent energies with these words. Nonetheless, it will not do at all for those not already absorbed in and attached to Homer, and able in some degree to use its complex subtleties in their construing of the Greek. But a version for general purposes must be a version for the Greekless. For them, the representation of Homer's language is almost all hindrance, encumbrance of the main undertaking by a minor historical-linguistic interest. *Thee*'s and *thou*'s, *thereof*'s *whereby*'s, *hath*'s, *doth*'s and *-eth*'s in general along with the nouns and adjectives of conscious archaism which match them, are better away. Their presence has become "the grievous bane"—to use a representative specimen—of translations in the Lang, Leaf, and Myers tradition.

Abandoning, then, all such scholarly verbal fidelity (which cost me no qualms since I could in no case aspire to it) I found myself embarrassingly free—as free as Chapman or Pope were—to pursue other aims. My other aims are obviously not theirs. They wrote in verse; I have written in what M. Jourdain was astonished to discover was prose. They wrote in a highly personal mode; I have, I hope, kept out of my sentences. It is a curious fact that these poets, when translating the *Iliad*, wrote most like themselves. Chapman is never more Chapman, Pope never more Pope, than there. Each reflects his age, no doubt; but each infects his age, too, and chiefly perhaps through his translation. Each, we may suppose, was writing as he thought verses should be written, less concerned to take a rubbing of Homer than to satisfy his own conception of an epic style. Writing not in verse but in some sort of general utility prose, I escape the influence of any such ideals and of many humbler literary aims as well. But I share their freedom from the Homeric form and the very modest scale of my endeavor gave me a wider freedom still. Let me now try to explain why, in view of what I have taken to be the chief general interest of the *Iliad*, I have limited the diction of this version as I have.

Let us consider briefly what possible publics there might be for a prose version of the *Iliad* in a moderately plain and fashion-free English. It is not customary to discuss these hypothetical matters in an introduction, but the circumstances call for full frankness here. The *Iliad* is a powerful instrument of propaganda which has been at work, off and on, through a very long time, with outcomes as to which there will naturally be disagreement. It is about aristocracy, was originally composed for aristocrats, and has always had most attention paid to it by aristocrats and as part of various programs of aristocratic education. It has frequently been rejected by aristocrats—Plato's *Republic* is the prime example—as exerting influences very undesirable in the training of aristocrats. It has on the whole been little known to those better placed than aristocrats can be to consider it more impersonally. It cannot be so considered while it is protected by a language, Greek or English, whose entrance price is a long and expensive literary education. And yet its main interest, as I have tried to suggest, is very far indeed from being anything that could rightly be an exclusive concern of any class. Moreover, before there can be a much wider knowledge and appraisal of the influences it sustains, a cleaning away of irrelevant incidents and insignificant accretions is necessary. The *Iliad* is choked with dense thickets of reported play-by-play fighting and celestial politics which commonly prevent the main sources of its power from being approached. I have tried to make such a clearance, to bring the plot out into the fullest clarity, and at the same time to parallel this clarification of the action with a simplification of the English I have used.

I am not taking sides in the great Homeric question, Is the *Iliad* the work of one poet or of many? That is an argument which now seems as artificial as the dispute over the shape of the fighters' shields. Writers on Homer have often felt it necessary to assume Achillean postures in these matters and perform feats of intellectual spearmanship. It is amusing evidence of the power of the poem upon them. Here, for example, is a particularly Pelean paragraph:

"I am anxious to find common ground with my unitarian critics. I only differ irreconcilably from those who reject all analysis *ab initio;* who assume as an unquestioned starting-point that, towards the end of the second millennium B.C., when to the best of our knowledge there was no Greek literature, a single miraculously gifted man, of whose life we know nothing, living in the heart of a rich, widespread, and romantic civilization, which no history mentions and all excavation has signally failed to discover, composed for an audience unable to read two poems much too long to be listened to; and then managed by miraculous but unspecified means to secure that his poems should be preserved practically unaltered while flying *viva per ora virum* through some six extraordinarily changeful centuries. . . ." [1]

That is a spear-fling from the semi-final round. Probably the question needs to be restated and be rather: What sequences can we *select* from this great body of composition? Which of them yields the best poem? Which of them serve best as tools in historical, anthropological, psychological speculation? This version is quite clearly an experiment in aesthetic selection, free to discard duplications, which are many, and whatever accretions seem to disturb the sought-for form. The *Iliad* as a digging site of materials for the historian and the *Iliad* as the most influential poem in the

[1] Gilbert Murray, *The Rise of the Greek Epic*, Preface to the Second Edition, 1911.

[17]

Western tradition should not be confused. They have different orders of endurance as Shakespeare takes such pains so often to point out. Action remains unchanged

> When time is old and hath forgot itself,
> When water drops have worn the stones of Troy,
> And blind oblivion swallow'd cities up,
> And mighty states characterless are grated
> To dusty nothing.
>
> *Troilus and Cressida* III, ii, 192

I have therefore been appropriately ruthless in cutting down the text in the interest of the action. Four whole Books (2, 10, 13, 17) and passages long and short from many of the others have been omitted. There is a strong continuing action to be found in the *Iliad*, but it is my experience that relatively few readers find or follow it. Book 2, for example, is an obstacle which eliminates, I would guess, half the starters. It contains nothing which bears on later events, and its main ingredients are a meaningless vacillation in Agamemnon which has no outcome and two long catalogs of the Greek and Trojan forces of interest only to specialists. One character, however, Thersites, makes his brief and only appearance here, memorable chiefly for what Shakespeare did with him. Book 10, similarly, is an excursion which interrupts and conflicts with the action, though it is a good independent story, distinct in character. Book 13, which chiefly celebrates the prowess of the Cretan hero Idomeneus, and Book 17, the endless struggle over Patroclus' body, I have not included, since they belong, I think, with the sections I have omitted in the other books, either as over-indulging the appetite of the Homeric audience for spear-flingings and woundings, or as pampering its taste for inter-ventions by the gods multiplied until interest is lost in com-plexity. The same principles have guided these large-scale decisions and my attempts to disencumber my version of everything in diction or in construction which could im-pede communication.

I have had another aim in mind in this control over syntax and vocabulary. The *Iliad* is in the most eminent degree world literature. English is at present the nearest thing there has yet been to a world language. I have let regard for those whose only access to the *Iliad* will be through the English they have learned as a second language weigh fairly heavily in my choices. But this is not a text designed mainly for the foreign student of English. It is a text for the widest range of readers—whether their English is native or acquired, and whether their interests are literary or just human—who find in its chief interest, as I outlined it above, an echo of their own.

But there is yet a further extension of these highly hypo-thetical publics to be considered. The *Iliad*, if it is made linguistically accessible, concerns all who need to under-stand the culture of which it is—along with the Bible and Plato—a principal source. Understanding a culture, in this sense, is no theoretical matter. It is understanding the behav-ior and attitudes of those who live by the culture—under-standing these in the sense of being able to guess what they will be. Countless people have lived and live by that culture who have never heard of the *Iliad*. Nonetheless, fundamental things in their behavior and attitudes, in what they do and how they feel and what they give up for what, and how they see themselves and others, can, I have suggested, be studied economically and profitably through the *Iliad*. I doubt that any contemporary English or American fiction or poetry can, in an equal time, help a Chinese, for example, to as clear and just a view of these things in the contemporary Englishman or American. For the *Iliad* contains the elements and can present them more intelligibly, because more simply, than in the complex current hybrid. But to do so the English version must have undergone its own appropriate simplification.

This public which needs to understand the Western culture contains, for every present English speaker, five or six people who know no English as yet. A considerable proportion of these are fated (cataclysms apart) to learn to read some English before the century ends. Their presence, on or just below the horizon, can reasonably be kept in mind. Those who are going to learn English should find things of permanent value to read early in their progress. But this influence of the foreign learner's needs is, in the case of the *Iliad*, surprisingly slight. The version which best serves the more general aim will, I think, best serve him, too. We may note, though, how well suited to his early reading the *Iliad* can be, with its repetitions, its low intake of new words after the first few pages, its extraordinarily clear action patterns and the surface simplicity of its motivation.

The choice of vocabulary, though it has its analogies with

the setting up of a palette, covers only a part of the problems of diction. It does not settle, for example, how ornate a version should be. Even with a severely limited vocabulary we have still to decide how often Hector shall be "flashing-helmeted Hector" or "horse-taming Hector" instead of just Hector; or Athene be "bright-eyed," or Hera "white-armed." I have been guided by two considerations in all this. The *Iliad* is highly ornate, as elaborately embroidered as the helmet strap beneath Paris' chin which would have put an end both to him and to the *Iliad*, in Book III, if it had only been tougher. There is a certain over-all contrast between the decorative manner and the stark facts recounted on which much of the effect of the *Iliad* depends, and I have put in enough ornament, I hope, to keep this contrast living. Secondly, every reader of the *Iliad* is struck, I think, by the different functions this decoration has in different places. Sometimes even the stock epithet will interact vigorously, if we let it, with the context. When wounded Diomede prays to Athene as "untiring one," there is a relevance of the epithet to his own situation which is quite absent in most such descriptions. So, too, with many, though not all, of the occasions in which Zeus is "bringer of clouds"; he is there deliberately making matters still more confused than they were. So, too, when the discomforted and panic-stricken Ares is described as "tireless of war" in Book 5. There is an irony here which we miss in other descriptions of Ares. Indeed, after his poor showing under Diomede's spear, we are apt to find a description of Aeneas, say, as "the equal of Ares" rather a poor compliment. All this may show how mixed and unstable the poets' attitudes to war were. But most of the inactive decoration comes, no doubt, from the conditions of oral metrical composition and I have as a rule given preference to ornament which has some noticeable relevance to what is going forward.

Modern readers expect discernible relevance where the audiences of the *Iliad* did not, and we are often unnecessarily troubled by its absence. In the great similes, for example, the development of the detail often seems to us to go directly against what we may suppose to be the point of the comparison. In Book 18 Athene puts a flame upon Achilles' head as he goes out to scare the Trojans. It is compared in the simile to the signal fires a besieged city may light to summon possible allies to its aid. There could hardly be a bigger contrast between the purposes of the two fires. And later on, in Book 19 when Achilles takes up his new shield, its gleam is compared to the light of a fire burning high up by a lonely hut on a mountain, which seamen who are being blown out to sea against their will by storm may gaze back to with anguish. This, too, if we are looking for demonstrable relevance—the sort of thing a footnoter can analyze—may still strike us as extraneous decoration, beautiful in itself but not taking part in the action. Many similar examples will be found. My own feeling is that if we must *think* about such matters, as the audiences of the *Iliad* almost certainly did not, we will do well to think further and not cut down relevance to connections we can reflectively perceive. I have been careful in my simplifications not to simplify such things out. Perhaps a wider knowledge of Homer might help poets back to a freedom which analytic criticism can seem to deny them. Much more can be said than the discursive script-ridden intellect can follow.

This saving reflection has often stood by me in more routine sorts of decision—as to word-order and the powers of inversion. No one has worked out the rhetorical differences between "I will arm now," "Now I will arm," and "I will now arm"; but no one can doubt their importance. When such choices turn up in every other sentence and govern as much as anything else the whole consistency, atmosphere, and movement, a writer is forced to recognize the incompleteness of his own understanding of the language he nominally possesses. And the simpler the form of the language the more such marginal differences probably affect the result. A would-be simple prose is especially troubled by imponderable choices. Departure from normal word-order is, of course, the most characteristic feature of most verse. Just when and where it is forced upon language by verse form and is not rather a *use* by verse of the rhetorical devices of speech is one of the most delicate of all questions. In rendering poetry into a prose which has deliberately renounced variety, this delicacy becomes excessive. Feeling has to resume supremacy over reflective judgment. Only the very broadest considerations can be handled by judgment. A plain business-letter sort of word-order throughout will not do; and a habitual inversion will not do—easy though it is to fall into that habit. But the mixtures and transitions are subject to no such rulings. They have to be left to the same nameless guide that prefers a more marked rhythm to a conversational tone sometimes, or decides that Athene must "give counsel" to the Greeks rather than "make serviceable suggestions" to them, as Samuel Butler would have her do.

But the greatest difficulties of all concern unity of tone. This same nameless guide has so many and such different things to do, and is so much influenced by the verbal company it has been keeping. It has very different standards as it comes to its work fresh from the newspaper or from Milton, from Fielding, James Joyce, or Hemingway. And the reader, too, who opens these pages comes to them with preparations diverse beyond conjecture. Much depends also on which page he opens. I have ventured—bethinking me of impetuous valor—to make the gods and goddesses talk a far more colloquial English than Achilles, and Pandarus in Book 5 has a similar license. The steps that slope down from this toward a version in truly contemporary English are slippery and I have not been tempted. To change the image, I have felt that such a version, though it would be more "readable" in a sense, would be too open to what communication theory calls *noise:* "additions to the signal not intended by the information source."

All through, in fact, I have been haunted by the engineer's diagram of a communication system. Here it is opposite.[1]

Here Homer (whatever that may be) is the *information source*. I (certain subsystems, rather, in me) am the *transmitter*. I encode certain things my information source seems

[1] From *The Mathematical Theory of Communication* by Claude E. Shannon and Warren Weaver, University of Illinois Press, Urbana, 1949, pp. 5 and 98.

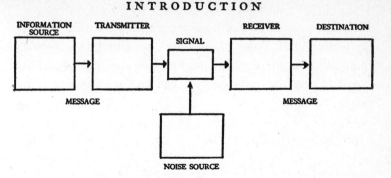

to give me in a *signal* which keeps up through the printed pages that follow. You (certain subsystems, rather, in you) are the *receiver*. You take in the marks on the paper which you recode again as sentences and hand on to the *destination*. This destination is the part of the diagram that has most of the appropriate poetic indefiniteness. It balances the mystery of the source which was "Homer." Whither, indeed, is all this directed? We have no better answer to give than Homer had. And as we wonder about that, the importance of the *noise source* needs no stressing—here, in the context of the first of all the poems which

> have power to make
> Our noisy years seem moments in the being
> Of the eternal Silence.

Further reflection on this diagram makes us aware that its great central gap is repeated; that between the information source and the transmitter, between the receiver and the destination, as between the transmitter and the receiver, come the noises—with an iteration most incident to hollow men.

It has been my hope that by a certain simplification imposed on what I took from Homer and by a certain generality imposed upon my signal, I might diminish these noises. But I realize that the real enemy I contend with is a taste for noise.

Hong Kong, 1950   I.A.R.

A LIST OF GODS, GODDESSES, GREEKS AND TROJANS

GODS AND GODDESSES

Zeus, son of Cronos, King of gods and ruler of the sky.

Poseidon, son of Cronos, King of the sea; on the side of the Greeks.

Hades, son of Cronos, ruler of the underworld of the dead.

Hera, daughter of Cronos; wife of Zeus; on the side of the Greeks.

Athene, daughter of Zeus; on the side of the Greeks.

Apollo, son of Zeus; on the side of the Trojans.

Aphrodite, daughter of Zeus; on the side of the Trojans.

Ares, son of Zeus; on the side of the Trojans.

Hephaestus, son of Zeus and Hera; on the side of the Greeks.

Hermes, son of Zeus; on the side of the Trojans.

Iris, messenger of the gods.

Thetis, a sea goddess, wife of Peleus and mother of Achilles.

GREEKS

Agamemnon, son of Atreus; King of Argos and Mycenae.

Menelaus, son of Atreus, King of Sparta or Lacedaemon; husband of Helen.

Achilles, son of Peleus and Thetis.

Nestor, son of Neleus.

Odysseus, son of Laertes.

Ajax, son of Telamon.

Diomede, son of Tydeus.

Patroclus, son of Menoetius.

Phoenix, teacher of Achilles.
Kalchas, a seer.
Machaon, a surgeon.
Talthybius and Eurybates, heralds.

TROJANS

Priam, son of Laomedon, King of Troy.
Hector, son of Priam.
Paris, son of Priam.
Helenus, son of Priam; a seer.
Deiphobus, Lycaon, and Polydorus, sons of Priam.
Sarpedon, son of Zeus; chief of the Lycians.
Glaucon, son of Hippolochus; a Lycian.
Aeneas, son of Anchises and Aphrodite; chief of the Dardanians.
Pandarus, a bowman.
Polydamas, counselor to Hector.
Idaeus, a herald.
Hecuba, wife of Priam; Queen of Troy.
Helen, wife of Menelaus; brought by Paris to Troy.
Andromache, daughter of Eëtion; wife of Hector.

THE
ILIAD
OF
HOMER

1

SING, goddess, the anger of Achilles, the anger which caused so many sorrows to the Greeks. It sent to Hades many souls of heroes and gave their bodies to be food of dogs and birds. So the design of Zeus was worked out from the time when, first, Agamemnon, king of men, and great Achilles were parted in anger.

Who of the gods did this? Apollo. He sent a plague into the Greek army because Agamemnon had wronged Chryses, his priest. For the priest came to their ships with gifts to free Chryseis, his daughter, taken by the Greeks in war. In his hands were the signs that he was priest to Apollo, the Archer, and he made this prayer to all the Greeks: "The gods send that you take Troy, and come back safe to your homes—but free my dear daughter and take these gifts in exchange—for fear of the son of Zeus, Apollo the Archer!"

Then all the rest of the Greeks cried out: "Hear the priest. Take the gifts." But this did not please Agamemnon who sent Chryses roughly away, saying: "Let me not see you, old man, near the hollow ships, waiting about now or coming back later. Being a priest may not keep you safe from me, if I do. Your daughter I will not free. Before that, let old age come upon her in our house, in Argos, far from her country, as she walks up and down before the loom and serves my bed. Go in peace! Do not make me angry!"

The old man went from him full of fear and in silence walked by the edge of the loud-sounding sea. When he had gone some distance he made this prayer to Apollo: "Hear me, god of the silver bow. Ruler over Chryse and Cilla and Tenedos, O Mouse-god! If ever I burned fat offerings to you give me now my desire. Let the Greeks pay through your arrows for my tears."

And Phoebus Apollo heard his prayer. He came down from the mountains of Olympus angry at heart, his bow and arrows on his shoulders shaking as he moved; and his coming was like the night. He let an arrow fly and the sound of his silver bow was fearful. First it was the mules and dogs his arrows killed and after that the men—till the fires of the dead were burning night and day.

For nine days his arrows killed. On the tenth day Achilles had the chiefs come to the meeting place—for the goddess, white-armed Hera, put this in his heart. She had sorrow for the Greeks, seeing so many of them dead. There Achilles stood and said: "Let us now hear from some priest, or from a reader of dreams (for dreams too are from Zeus), why Apollo is so angry. What have we done? What can we give him to take this plague away?"

So he said, and sat down; and then Kalchas stood before them—Kalchas, far the best of the seers who knew things past and present and to come. It was Kalchas who had guided the Greek ships to Troy by the knowledge Apollo gave him. And these were his words: "Achilles, you would have me tell why Apollo, the Archer, is angry. And I will; but take thought and swear now to help me. For what I say will anger one who rules over all the Greeks. What can such a man as I do against a king? Though he keep down his anger and wait before paying me back? Think now. Will you keep me safe?"

Then swift-footed Achilles answered: "Fear not, Kalchas, but tell what you know. For by Apollo himself, through whom you have your knowledge, no man, while I live and see the light on earth, is going to put violent hands upon you among these hollow ships—no man of all the Greeks, no, not Agamemnon himself who now says he is the greatest by far of them all."

Then Kalchas took heart and said: "It is because of Chryses—priest of Apollo—because Agamemnon wronged him and would not free Chryseis his daughter or take his gifts, that Apollo does this to us; and he will do more still. He will not stop the plague till we have given bright-eyed Chryseis freely back to her father but without gifts in exchange now, and we must send a great and holy offering to Chryse. Then, it may be, the Archer will hear our prayer."

So he said and sat down, and then stood up before them wide-ruling Agamemnon the King. His dark heart within him was full of anger and his eyes were like fire. "Seer of evil," he cried, "never yet did you tell of any good thing. And is this why the plague is among us? Because I would not give back this girl Chryseis? I would not; for she is better in my eyes than even my wife Clytemnestra—as beautiful, as tall, as skillful and as wise. Nonetheless, I will give her back. I would have the people safe, not dead. Only make ready for me in her place an equal prize. I will not be the only one of the Greeks to be without his prize of honor. You see how my prize is being taken from me."

At that swift-footed Achilles answered: "Great King Agamemnon, most profit-loving of men, how can the Greeks give you a prize? We have no common store. What we got from the cities we took has been divided, and we cannot now ask for it back. But do you give up this girl to her father, at Apollo's word, and we will pay you three or four times over whenever Zeus lets us take well-walled Troy."

Then Agamemnon said: "Strong you may be, godlike Achilles, but you will not trick me like this. What! Will you tell me to give my prize up, and am I to be without one while you keep yours? No! If the great-hearted Greeks will give me another prize, one pleasing to me and equal to my honor, good! But if not, then I, myself, will go and take a prize of honor—from you or from Ajax or Odysseus— and angry will he be to whom I come. But of this later.

First let a black ship be made ready to put to sea and journey to Chryse with fair-faced Chryseis and the offerings. So may we be at peace with Apollo whose arrows fly so far."

Then swift-footed Achilles looked at him angrily and said: "O you without shame, how can any Greek do your will with any heart either to journey or to fight! It was not because of the Trojan spearmen that I came to this war. They never did me any wrong, never took my cattle or horses, or cut down my harvest in deep-soiled Phthia. For many things stretch between us, shadowy mountains and sounding sea. It was for you, you without shame, that we came here, to make the Trojans pay—for Menelaus and for you, you dog-face! But you think nothing now of that. You would take my prize of honor, would you, for which I fought and which the Greeks gave to me! My reward when we take a town is never as great as yours, though it is my hands which do the fighting. But now I will sail back to Phthia with my ships. It is better than going on fighting here without honor to get you more treasure and gold."

Then Agamemnon the King answered Achilles: "Run away if you will. I will not ask you to stay. I have others to honor me and, highest of all, Zeus, Lord of counsel. What if you are strong, does not that come to you from heaven? Go home now with your ships and company and lord it among your Myrmidons. What do I care for you or your anger? And know this: because Phoebus Apollo is taking away my Chryseis, I myself will come to your hut and take away your prize of honor, even fair-faced Briseis, so that you may see how much greater I am than you. Then others, in time to come, may be slower to match themselves with me."

So he said, and sorrow came upon Achilles, and his heart within him was divided between taking out his sword to kill Agamemnon and controlling his anger. While he was still in two minds about it and was putting his hand to his great sword, Athene came to him from Heaven, sent by the white-armed goddess Hera, who had love and care in her heart for Agamemnon and Achilles both. And Athene came and took Achilles by his golden hair. Now she was seen by him only and by none of the others. And Achilles turned about and knew who it was and her eyes were terribly bright. Then he said: "Why do you come here now, daughter of Zeus? Is it to see how Agamemnon pays for his pride with his life?"

Then bright-eyed Athene said: "I came from Heaven, sent by white-armed Hera who has love and care in her heart for you both. So take your hand from that sword and let him be. I tell you now that gifts three times as great will come to you through this act of his. But with words, if you will, attack him."

And swift-footed Achilles answered: "Goddess! A man must do as the two of you say, however angry he is. The gods hear those who do their will."

So Athene went back to the other gods in the house of Zeus on Olympus and Achilles turned again and let loose his anger against Agamemnon in bitter words. "You full wineskin, you; you with the face of a dog and the heart of a fawn. You never arm yourself to fight for your people.

That would seem as bad as death to you! Much better, is it not, to take for yourself the prize of honor of every man who has a word to say against you? But I will say this and swear a great oath to back it. By this staff we take in our hands as we give judgment, by this staff which will never be green again or have branches or leaves, for the ax has cut them from it, by this witness to the rule of Heaven itself—there will come a time when every man of the Greeks will look long for Achilles to help him. Much help will you be to them then, for all your sorrow, as they fall before man-killing Hector. In that day you will bite on your heart in your anger because you did this wrong to the best of the Greeks."

So said Achilles, and down on the earth between them he threw the gold-nailed staff and took his seat while Agamemnon became still angrier. Then between them stood Nestor of the clear voice from whose lips came words sweeter than honey. He was an old man and had seen much. He said: "With this a great sorrow comes upon the Greeks. Truly Priam and his sons and all the Trojans would be happy to hear how you two—greatest of the Greeks in counsel and in the fighting—are now separated in anger. Hear me now, you are younger both than I am. In the old days I talked with better men even than you are, and they gave attention to what I said. They heard my voice. Do not, King Agamemnon, great though you are, take this girl from him. She was given to him by the Greeks as his prize of honor; and do not you, Achilles, attempt to have your way by force against a king. You are strong, no doubt, and your mother is a goddess; but still Agamemnon is greater than you, for he rules over more people. Agamemnon, keep down your anger, I pray you, and put an end to this, for Achilles is to all the Greeks our great defense in evil war."

And Agamemnon answered, "All you have said, old man, is quite true. But must this man be chief over all of us? The gods may have made him a spearman, but have they given him the right to talk to us so?"

Then Achilles cried out: "Yes, and may I be named a coward if I give way and do everything you tell me to do. You may give your orders to others. But take this to heart. I will not use force to keep the girl—not to you or to anyone; you gave her to me and now you take her away. But do not attempt to take away anything more that I have by my ship. If you do, all men will see how quickly your dark blood comes bursting out under my spear!"

When these two had ended their war of words, the meeting before the Greek ships broke up. Achilles went to his huts and Agamemnon put a good ship on the sea, with twenty seamen in her, and sent on board beautiful Chryseis and the offering for Apollo. Odysseus went with them as captain.

So these sailed over the wet ways; and Agamemnon ordered the people to make themselves clean. And they did, throwing whatever was dirty into the sea, and made offerings of cattle and goats to Apollo by the edge of the unharvested sea; and the sweet smell from the burning went up to Heaven in the twisting smoke.

Then Agamemnon sent two heralds to take fair-faced

Briseis, Achilles' prize of honor, from him. And he said to them: "Go to Achilles' hut and take fair-faced Briseis by the hand and come back here with her; and if he will not give her up to you, then I will go myself and many men with me and take her, and that will be so much the more sorrow to him."

Unwillingly they went along the edge of the unresting sea, and when they came to Achilles' huts and ships they stood before him and said nothing. But he knew in his heart what they came for and cried: "Come near, O heralds. It is not you who do this wrong, but Agamemnon who sent you. Go now, Patroclus, and give the girl to them to take away. But let them be witnesses, before gods and men, and before that king of theirs, too, when later he needs me to save all the Greeks from destruction."

Patroclus gave the girl to them and they took their way back to Agamemnon's ships and unwillingly she went with them.

Then Achilles sat down by himself in tears at the edge of the gray sea, looking out across the endless waters; and he stretched out his hands and made this prayer to his goddess mother. "Mother. To a short life you bore me. And honor, at least, might Zeus, who thunders on high, have given me. But he does not. For wide-ruling Agamemnon has dishonored me. He has taken my prize of honor from me and by force he keeps her."

And Thetis, his mother, heard him and she came up out of the gray sea, like a mist, and sat by him and touched him with her hand and said: "My child, why are you crying?

What sorrow is in your heart? Do not keep it from me; tell me; let us both know it together."

Then Achilles said: "You know it well. Why do I tell it to you who know everything? We went against Thebe, the city of Eëtion, and took it. And the Greeks made a division and they gave beautiful Chryseis to Agamemnon as his prize. But Chryses, priest of Apollo the Archer, came to our ships for his daughter with gifts in exchange. In his hands were the signs that he was priest to Apollo and he made his prayer to all the Greeks. All the others cried out: 'Hear the priest and take the gifts.' But this did not please Agamemnon, who sent him roughly away. The old man went back in anger, and Apollo, who loved him, heard his prayer and took up his bow against the Greeks. He killed many. Then the seer, Kalchas, out of his full knowledge, told us how we had wronged Apollo, and I was the first to say what we had to do. But Agamemnon grew angry, and now he has done what he said. While Chryseis is sailing over the sea to Chryse, with offerings to Apollo, the heralds but now came and took from my hut the other, Briseis, whom the Greeks gave to me. So now, mother, help your son, if you can. Go now up to Olympus. If ever you made the heart of Zeus, Lord of the thunder cloud, happy, go to him now. For I have heard you tell in my father's house how you saved him once, when the other Olympians, Hera and Poseidon and Athene, were for putting him in chains. But you came and saved him, goddess, bringing Briareus of the hundred hands. And he sat down by Zeus' side, and the other gods were afraid of him and did not chain Zeus. Bring this back to his memory, and pray at his knees. Let him give help now to the Trojans. Let them drive the Greeks in among their very ships on the sand, killing them there. Let the Greeks see then what Agamemnon can do to help them, and let him, wide-ruling Agamemnon himself, know how blind he was when he dishonored the best of the Greeks."

And Thetis gave him her word to do so.

At Chryse, Odysseus gave back Chryseis to her father's arms. And they made their offerings with music to Apollo, singing to him all day long his own beautiful song, and their voices pleased his heart. When the sun went down and night came upon them, they slept by the side of the ship; and at the coming of rose-fingered Dawn, they sailed back again to the wide camp of the Greeks. And Apollo sent them the wind they desired. Out went their white sails, full of the wind, and the deep blue wave sang loudly about them as their ship went on her way. When they came to the wide camp of the Greeks, they pulled up their black ship high on the sand, and put strong supports under her; and they themselves went off to their own huts and ships.

But swift-footed Achilles, still in his anger, sat by the side of his swift ships and did not go either to the meeting, where men get honor, or into the battle. But there he waited, his heart broken with desire for the war cry and the fighting.

And Thetis went to Olympus and found Zeus sitting by himself away from the other gods, on the highest point of the mountain. And she sat down before him, taking his knees in her left hand and touching his chin with her right, and made her prayer to him as Achilles had desired.

But Zeus sat for a long time in silence, saying nothing. And Thetis made her prayer a second time. "Give me your word now and bend your head. Or say no—you have nothing to fear—so that I may learn how far I among all the gods am the least honored."

Then, in great trouble, Zeus, bringer of clouds, answered her. "This will make Hera angry, and me, too, when she says her say. Already she keeps telling me I am helping the Trojans in battle. But for the present go, and do not let Hera see you. And I will think over how these things may be done. See, I will bend my head to it so that you may believe me. This is the most certain sign I can give any god. I never take back any word to which I bend my head."

So saying, the son of Cronos bent his head, and the ambrosial hair waved; and he made great Olympus shake.

When the two had taken counsel together so, the goddess sprang down from Olympus into the deep sea and Zeus went to his own house. All the gods stood up together as he came in. And he took his seat. But Hera, when she saw him, knew that the silver-footed daughter of the old man of the sea had been with him, and said at once: "Who of the gods has been talking to you now? You never tell me your secrets, or what it is you are purposing to do."

The father of gods and men answered: "Hera, you must not think you have to know all my thoughts. You are my wife, it is true, but some of my decisions are hard. What it is right for you to know, I will tell you before any other, of gods or men. But do not ask me about things which I am minded to keep to myself."

To this, ox-eyed, queenly Hera answered: "Most dread son of Cronos, what is this? I never ask you questions. I let you design everything as you will in peace and quiet. But I am very much afraid that silver-footed Thetis, daughter of the old man of the sea, has been getting the better of you. She was sitting at your knees only this morning. You bent your head to her, I think, as a sign that you are going to bring many of the Greeks to death by their ships—all to honor Achilles."

Then the cloud-bringer said: "What has got into you now, queen? You are always having ideas and I have to hear them. But there is nothing you can do about it. You will only be the farther from me and that will not be so good for you. If things are as you say, then clearly that is my pleasure. So sit down in silence and do what I say, for all the gods in Olympus cannot help you, if I put my hands on you."

And Hera was afraid and she sat down in silence, keeping her anger down. Then the heavenly gods throughout the house of Zeus were troubled; till Hephaestus, to please white-armed Hera, his mother, said: "It will be impossible, if you two go on arguing like this about mortal men. There will be no joy at our feasts if this goes on. My counsel to my mother, wise as she is, is to please our dear father Zeus, so that he does not have to say any more and turn the feast into a fight. What if the Olympian, Lord of the lightning, takes to throwing us out of our seats! He is by far the strongest. So give him fair words and he will be in a good humor quickly again."

He sprang up and gave Hera a double cup of nectar, saying: "Take heart, mother. I do not want to see you being punished. I would not be able to help you, whatever I felt. There is no fighting with the Olympian. Once before, when I attempted to save you, he took me by the foot and threw me right out of Heaven. I went on falling head first all day, and there was not much life in me when I came to Lemnos at sundown. The Sintians took care of me after that."

Then Hera smiled and smiling took the cup. And Hephaestus poured wine for all the other gods from left to right. The gods laughed long to see Hephaestus at such work. So all day long till the going down of the sun they feasted, and their hearts were not short of anything at the equal feast; not of the lyre that Apollo held or the Muses that sang, their sweet voices answering one to another.

But when the bright light of the sun had gone, each went to his own house, built for him by Hephaestus, god of the two strong hands, to take his rest. And Zeus, the Olympian, Lord of the lightning, went to his bed where he rested when sweet sleep overcame him. He went there and slept with Hera at his side.

3

NOW ordered in companies under their chiefs, the Greeks and the Trojans went out to war. The Trojans came on with a noise like the crying of birds as they fly from the storms and endless rain of winter. But the Greeks came on in silence breathing angrily, and ready every man to give help one to another.

As when the South Wind brings a mist over the mountain-tops, bad for the shepherd but better than night for the robber, and a man can see no farther than he can throw a stone, so thick was the dust cloud from under their feet. And quickly they made their way across the plain.

When the two armies came near together, godlike Paris

came forward as a champion on the Trojan side. He had a mountain lion's skin on his shoulders, with his bow and his sword; and he was waving two bronze pointed spears and crying out to the best of the Greeks to meet him face to face in deadly fight.

When Menelaus saw him, out in front of the rest like this, he was as glad as a hungry lion is to see a goat, and he springs upon it though dogs and young men come against him. So glad was Menelaus to see godlike Paris before him. He thought he had got his payment now from the sinner. And he sprang down in his armor from his chariot.

But when godlike Paris saw him, his heart gave way, and he fell back among his men in fear of his life. As a man who sees a snake before him in a mountain hollow steps back, and back again, with white face and shaking knees, so did Paris fall back among the Trojans on seeing Menelaus.

Hector saw him and put shame upon him with these words: "Evil-hearted Paris, beautiful to look upon, woman-mad and false of tongue. How much better if you had never been! Better far than to bring shame on us like this. Now the long-haired Greeks will laugh and say that our beautiful hero has no heart in him or courage. Was it you who got your men together and sailed across the seas, and brought back Helen, a daughter of spearmen, to be a bitter evil to your father and city and all the people—to our enemies joy but to you a cause for hanging your head in shame? Is it too much to face Menelaus now, and learn what sort of man he is whose wife you took? You will get no help from your lyre, or from the gifts of Aphrodite, your beauty or your bright hair, when you are down in the dust before him. The Trojans are a softhearted people or long before this they would have given you a shirt of stones, for all the wrong you have done them."

And godlike Paris answered: "You are right enough, Hector. You are as hard as the ax in a shipbuilder's hand, so sharp your fearless heart is. Still do not throw in my teeth the beautiful gifts of golden Aphrodite. No man can put the gifts of the gods from him, which they themselves give; and no man by his own will can win them. But now, if you would have me fight Menelaus, make the other Trojans and Greeks all be seated, while he and I fight between them for Helen and all her treasure. And whichever of us wins, let him take it all and the woman. And as for you others, be friends again and swear peace together with offerings—you to live on in deep-soiled Troyland and they to go back home to Argos and the lands of the Greeks."

So he said, and Hector had great joy at his words. And he went between the armies holding his spear by the middle and keeping back the Trojans with it; and they sat down. But for a time arrows and stones kept coming at him from the long-haired Greeks, till Agamemnon, King of men, cried: "Hold, Greeks, for bright-helmeted Hector has something in his mind to say."

They stopped and were still. Then Hector cried: "Hear now, Trojans and Greeks, the words of Paris, through whom this war came upon us. He says, Let the other Trojans now, and the Greeks put down their arms on the fruitful earth. He himself and Menelaus, dear to Ares, will fight now for

Helen and all her treasure. Whichever of these two wins, let him take it all and the woman. And let the rest of us be friends again and swear an oath of peace together."

They were all silent. Then Menelaus said: "Hear me now, too, for into my heart most of all has sorrow come. Now at last, I think, the Greeks and Trojans may go their separate ways. You have undergone much through my wrong and the sin of Paris. For whichever of us death and fate are waiting, let him die; and the rest fight no more. Now bring two young sheep, one white, one black, for Earth and Sun; and for Zeus another. And send to Troy for great Priam, so that he may swear this peace before the offerings himself. His sons are highhanded and no keepers of their word. It is wrong to break oaths to Zeus. Young men's hearts change quickly, but an old man looks before and after, so that the outcome may be best for both sides."

So he said, and the Greeks and Trojans were glad, thinking that rest from war was coming. So they lined their chariots back and took off their armor and put it down on the earth. There was little space between. And Hector sent heralds to the city to bring the lambs and Priam. And Agamemnon sent his herald, Talthybios, to the hollow ships to bring a lamb.

Now Iris, making herself like Laodice, Helen's sister-in-law, the best-looking of Priam's daughters, went to Helen. She found her in her own house, working at a great cloth picture, threading into it the battles of the horse-taming Trojans and the bronze-coated Greeks. Iris came to her side and said: "Come with me now, Helen, and see the strange doings of the horse-taming Trojans and bronze-coated Greeks. Till now, they have been warring upon the plain, their hearts full of deadly battle. But now they are seated resting on their shields with their long spears planted by their sides. Paris and Menelaus are going to fight for you, and whoever wins, his wife you are to be."

So said the goddess, and put into Helen's heart sweet thoughts of Menelaus, and of her father and mother and her city. So she covered her head with white linen and went out in tears, and her two handmaids went with her and quickly they came to the Scaean gates.

And there over the gates the old men of the people were seated with Priam. They were too old now for fighting, but very good at talking. And there they were, seated up on the wall like cicadas up in a tree, keeping their voices going. Now when they saw Helen coming up on the wall, they said softly to one another: "Little blame is it that Trojans and Greeks have undergone so much so long for such a woman. Unbelievably like the immortal goddesses she is to look upon! But still, whatever she is, let her go away with their ships, and not bring sorrow to us and our children after us."

And Priam said to her: "Come, dear child, and take a seat in front of me where you can see your husband that was and your friends and people. The blame is not yours, in my eyes, but the gods', who brought this war upon me."

And Helen answered: "Great and dear to me, father of my lord, O that evil death had been my pleasure before I came here with your son, far away from Menelaus' bed and my loved daughter and the friends I had as a girl. But that was not to be, and it is tears I have to live by. And now I see all the Greeks before me. But two I do not see, Castor and Polydeuces, my brothers. It may be they did not come with the rest from beautiful Lacedaemon, or they have no heart now to come into the battle for fear of the shame I am to them."

She did not know that they were both under the earth in their own dear Lacedaemon.

But now the heralds were bringing the offerings through the city, the two lambs and a goatskin of wine, fruit of the earth, which makes the heart glad. And a herald came to the old king's side, saying: "Son of Laomedon, the chiefs of the horse-taming Trojans and the bronze-coated Greeks wait for you to go down into the plain and swear an oath for them before the offerings. Paris and Menelaus are to fight with long spears for Helen, and whichever of the two is the winner, with him she is to go. And we others then will live on in deep-soiled Troy, but they will go back to Argos and the lands of the Greeks."

The old man shook at his words, but gave his orders to put horses to his chariot, and quickly they did so. Then he stepped in and took the reins and Antenor went with him, driving down through the Scaean gates to the plain. When they came to the Trojans and Greeks, they got down and went into the space between them. Then Agamemnon came forward and with him Odysseus; and the heralds brought together the offerings to the gods and mixed the wine and poured water over the kings' hands. And Agamemnon took his knife which was hanging by the side of his great sword and cut hair from the lambs' heads. And the heralds gave it out to the chiefs of the Trojans and Greeks. Then Agamemnon lifted up his hands and made this prayer: "Father Zeus, you who rule from Ida, most glorious, most great; and you, O Sun, seer and hearer of all things; and you Rivers and you, O Earth; and you who under earth punish after their lives men who swear false oaths, be witnesses now and watch that what we swear now we keep unbroken. If Paris kills Menelaus, let him keep Helen and all that is hers; and we will go away in our ships. But if fair-haired Menelaus kills Paris, let the Trojans give back Helen and all her treasure and pay to the Greeks what is right as the price of sin, a price to be kept in mind by men now unborn. But if Priam and his sons will not pay this price when Paris falls, then I will fight on till I win it and so put an end to war."

So he said and cut the lambs' throats with the pitiless knife; and he put them down on the earth, without breath, for the knife had taken their strength from them. Then they took the wine in their cups and poured it and prayed to the gods who are forever. And one or other of the Greeks and Trojans would say: "Zeus, most glorious, most great, and all you undying gods, whichever army is the first to sin, may their brains be poured out on the earth like this wine, theirs and their children's; and may their wives become slaves to others."

Then Priam said: "Hear me, Trojans and Greeks. I am going back to windy Troy. To watch my dear son fighting with Menelaus would be more than I can do. But Zeus knows, and the other immortal gods, to which of the two his death is fated."

So the godlike man said, and had the lambs placed in his chariot, and got in and took up the reins and Antenor got in with him and the two went back to Troy. But Hector and Odysseus measured out a space and put the lots in a bronze helmet to be shaken to decide which of the two was to throw his spear first. And the people prayed and lifted their hands to the gods and one or other of the Trojans or Greeks would say: "Father Zeus, you rule from Ida, most glorious, most great, whichever of the two brought these troubles upon both people, may he die and go down to the house of Hades, but to us may peace and goodwill come."

Great Hector now shook the bronze helmet, turning his eyes away from it, and the lot of Paris came out first. Then the people were quickly seated each by his horses and the place where his arms were, while Paris, lord of fair-haired Helen, put on his beautiful armor. First he put well-made guards on his legs; then on his chest a breastplate; and about his shoulders he hung his silver-worked sword of bronze and his great strong shield; and upon his head he put a well-hammered helmet with its horsehair crest—fearfully did the crest wave down—and he took a strong spear the right size for his hands. And Menelaus in the same way put on his armor.

When they were both ready they went into the space between the armies and took their places near together in the measured space, shaking their spears angrily at one another. First Paris threw his far-shadowing spear, and hit Menelaus' shield, but the bronze point was turned by the strong shield and did not break through. Then Menelaus lifted up his spear with this prayer to father Zeus: "Zeus, O King, let me now pay back fair Paris, who wronged me. Put him now in my hands; so that men to come may shake with fear at the thought of doing a wrong to their host."

So saying, he threw, and hit Paris' shield; through the bright shield the spear went, and through the breastplate and through his shirt, at his side—but he turned and kept black death away. Then Menelaus took his sword and hit the horn of Paris' helmet, but the sword was broken into three or four bits in his hand. Then looking up into wide Heaven, Menelaus bitterly cried: "Father Zeus, not one of the gods is crueller than you. I thought I had Paris in my hands, but my sword has broken in my hand and I have thrown my spear, and I have not killed him."

With that he sprang on Paris and took him by the horse-hair crest of his helmet and twisted him round and started to drag him toward the Greeks. The tight ornamented strap of the helmet cut off Paris' breath in his soft throat; and Menelaus would have dragged him away and won untold glory, if Aphrodite, daughter of Zeus, had not been quick to see. She broke the strap and the helmet came away hollow in Menelaus' strong hand. He threw it clear away to his company among the Greeks, who took it up, and sprang back himself to kill Paris with his spear. But Aphrodite lifted Paris up, as a goddess may, covering him round with thick cloud, and put him down in his sweet-smelling room in Troy and went herself to look for Helen.

She found her on the high wall with the women of Troy all round her. In the form of an old woman, a wool-comber, well loved by Helen when she worked for her in Lacedaemon, she took hold of her sweet-smelling dress and shook it and said: "Come with me. Paris has sent for you to go home. There he is on his bed in his own room bright with beauty and fair linen. You would not think he had come there from the fight but that he was going to a dance or resting from it."

So she said, and moved Helen's heart within her breast. And Helen looked and noted the beautiful neck and breast and the bright eyes of the goddess, and saw her for what she was and said: "Strange, goddess; why would you trick me so? Would you send me now to some man you have taken up in Phrygia or fair Maeonia? For Menelaus has overcome Paris and I must go with him, hated though I am, to his home. You have come to me here for no good. Go and be with Paris yourself. Be a goddess no longer; never again let your feet take you back to Olympus, but care for him and look after him till he makes you his wife or, maybe, his slave. I will not go to him—for shame—to ornament that man's bed. All the women of Troy will blame me. And I have measureless sorrow in my heart."

Then fair Aphrodite said: "Move me not to anger, thoughtless woman, or I may hate you even as I now love you, and what then would be your end?"

Fear took hold of Helen, and she covered her head with the bright white linen and went in silence, unseen by the Trojan women, and the goddess went before.

When they came to the beautiful house of Paris, the hand-maids turned to their work, but Helen went into Paris' high-roofed room. And laughter-loving Aphrodite brought a seat and put it for her facing Paris. There Helen, daughter of Zeus, seated herself with eyes turned to one side, and said to her lord: "So you are back from the war. Why were you not killed there by that great fighter who was my husband? You used to say you were a better man than Menelaus, stronger with your hands and your spear. Go then and get Menelaus to fight you again man to man. But maybe you will be wiser not to, or it will not be long before he kills you with his spear."

And Paris answered: "Send no more such words through my heart, Helen. Menelaus has overcome me now with Athene's help; but I may do the same to him another day, for I too have gods on my side. Come now, let us take our joy together in love. Never before has desire so held my heart —no, not even when I first took you away from beautiful Lacedaemon and I sailed with you on my ships and in the island of Cranaë we came together in love—so much now I love you and sweet desire takes hold of me." Saying so, he went before her to the bed and Helen with him.

So the two were together on the corded bed. But Menelaus ran up and down among the armies looking everywhere for godlike Paris. But no one, of the Trojans or their allies, had any news of him. Not for love were they covering him up, for he was hated by them all like black death. Then Agamemnon, King of men, said among them: "Hear me, Trojans and Dardanians and allies. Menelaus has been the winner.

Give back Helen, then, and all her treasure, and pay us more-over what is right so that men unborn may keep in mind the price of sin."

So said Agamemnon and all the Greeks cried that he was right.

4

╟═══╢

THE GODS were seated with Zeus in his golden
house and Hebe poured them their nectar. Lift-
ing their golden cups they drank to one another
looking out upon Troy. And to make Hera angry
Zeus said: "Menelaus has two of the goddesses for helpers,
Hera and Athene, but they only sit still and look on while
laughter-loving Aphrodite is always by Paris' side, keeping
off fate; and now she has saved him when he thought he
would be killed. Menelaus is truly the winner. What then
are we to do about it: start the war again, or make peace be-
tween the armies? If you will all agree, the Trojans can go
on living in Troy and Menelaus take back Helen."

Athene and Hera were sitting side by side designing evil for the Trojans. Athene said nothing, angry though she was at father Zeus, but Hera could not keep her anger down. "Dread son of Cronos," she said, "what is this? Is all my trouble then to come to nothing, all the work I and my horses had in getting the Greeks together against Priam and his children? Do what you will, but know that we other gods are not all with you in this."

Moved to hot anger, Zeus answered: "What is in you, goddess! What have Priam and his sons done to you to make you desire so much to waste their well-built city? Must you go inside their gates and high walls and eat Priam raw, and his sons and all the other Trojans, before you are happy? Have it your own way. This is not to become a cause for more fighting between us. But I will say this, and take it to heart, please. If I ever desire to waste a city where your friends live, do not attempt to stop me. You must let me do it, for I am giving in to you now much against my will. Of all the cities under the sun and the stars of Heaven, this Troy I honored most."

And Hera answered: "I have three cities which are dearest in my sight: Argos, Sparta, and wide-wayed Mycenae. Waste these whenever they are hateful to your heart. So let us give way to one another in this, and all the other gods will do the same. Now send Athene down to make the Trojans be the first to break their oath and attack the joyful Greeks."

Down from Olympus went Athene, like a bright shooting star, and the horse-taming Trojans and bronze-coated

Greeks saw her and wondered. And a man would look at another and say: "Are we to have evil war and the dread noise of fighting again, or will Zeus, Lord of battle, now make peace between us?"

Athene, looking like Laodocus, son of Antenor, a good spearman, went up to Pandarus and said: "Wise-hearted Pandarus, why not let fly a swift arrow now at Menelaus and win great glory in the eyes of all the Trojans and King Paris most of all? What will he not give you to see Menelaus killed by your arrow?"

So she said and moved the foolish man's heart with her words. He uncovered his polished horn bow, and made it ready. And the Trojans in front of him held up their shields so that the Greeks could not see what he was doing. He put an arrow, never used before, to the string, gripping both the arrow and the string. He bent the bow and brought the string to his breast and the iron arrowhead to the bow. Then he let fly and the string sang as the arrow flew over men's heads.

The gods kept you in mind, Menelaus, then. Athene turned away the arrow as a mother will drive a fly away from her sleeping child. She guided it to where his armor was thickest, but right through it all the arrow went. It cut his outer skin only and blood came springing up from the wound.

When Agamemnon saw the dark blood he shook with fear. So did Menelaus himself till he saw that the arrowhead was outside the wound. Then his spirit came back into his breast again. With a heavy moan Agamemnon took Menelaus' hand—and the Greeks about them moaned too. "Dear brother," he said, "I have caused your death by swearing this oath. But not for nothing are the oath, the blood of lambs, the drink offerings, and all the rest in which we believed. If he who rules on Olympus does not always act here and now, men pay the price later with their own heads and their wives and children. I know this now in heart and soul: The day will come for Troy and Priam and the people of Priam when Zeus himself will shake over them his dark aegis in punishment for this."

But Menelaus said: "Take heart. The arrow has touched no deadly place."

And Agamemnon answered: "May it be so. But a surgeon must see to the wound and put on it what will take away the pain." And he sent Talthybios the herald to bring Machaon, the best of all the surgeons. While they were helping Menelaus, the Trojans made ready and the Greeks armed themselves again to meet them.

As when at the edge of the sounding sea wave after wave comes up under the driving of the West Wind—out on the deep it lifts its crest and is broken on the land with a noise like thunder and far over the headlands shoots its salt foam —so did the Greek lines then go into battle. Each chief gave his men their orders, but the rest said not a word. You would not have thought that all that great army had a voice among them, in such silence they all went through fear of their chiefs. And as they moved, the armor upon their bodies flashed in the sun. But the Trojans—as sheep in thousands at the farm of some rich man, waiting to be milked of their white milk, baa without end to the baaing of their lambs—the Trojans made an endless noise throughout their army. For they had no one language, their tongues were many, they were peoples brought together from many lands.

5

NOW Pallas Athene gave great strength and courage
to Diomede, that he might outdo all the other
Greeks and cover himself with glory. You could
not have seen which army he was joined with,
Greek or Trojan. For he raged across the plain like a winter
river at the full, which has broken through its banks. No
banks or walls of fruitful vineyards can hold it or stop its
sudden coming when rain from Heaven drives it on, and
many of the fair works of man go down before it. So before
Diomede the lines of the Trojans were broken. They did
not wait for him though they were many.

When Pandarus saw him raging across the plain, driving
the Trojans before him, he bent his curved bow against him

and hit him near the right shoulder. The bitter arrow went straight through his breastplate, covering it with blood. Then loudly Pandarus cried: "Up now, greathearted Trojans! The best man of the Greeks is wounded. He will not hold out against my arrow long, if King Apollo was with me when I came here from Lycia."

So in his joy he cried. But the arrow had not killed Diomede. He went back to his horses and chariot, and Sthenelos his driver pulled the swift arrow clean through his shoulder. Then Diomede prayed to Athene: "Hear me, daughter of Zeus, untiring one. If ever you loved my father and helped him in battle, be kind to me now. Let me kill this man if he comes within the throw of my spear, this man who hit me before ever I saw him and now cries out that I am not to see the bright light of the sun for long."

And Pallas Athene heard his prayer and made his feet and hands strong. She came to his side and said: "Fear not, Diomede, to fight on. In your heart I have put the strength of your father, Tydeus. I have taken the mist from your eyes, moreover, to see and separate men from gods. If any god now comes against you, do not fight. Only if Aphrodite, Zeus' daughter, offers you battle, give her the sharp bronze and wound her well."

When she had said this, the goddess, flashing-eyed Athene, went away and Diomede came back into the battle with three times the courage that he had before. He was like a lion that a shepherd keeping his sheep in the field has wounded but not killed as he sprang over the wall; so now did Diomede fall on the Trojans.

When Aeneas saw him he went his way through the fight under the rain of spears looking everywhere for godlike Pandarus. He found him and said: "Where now, Pandarus, are your bow and your winged arrows and your name as an archer? There is no man your equal or any in Lycia better than you. Lift up your hands to Zeus now, and send an arrow into this man, whoever he is, that has loosed the knees of so many good men—if truly he is not some god who is angry with the Trojans; heavy is the anger of a god upon men."

Pandarus answered: "Aeneas, he looks to me very like Diomede in every way, by his shield and his crested helmet and his horses. And yet I do not know for certain that he is not a god. If he is wise-hearted Diomede and the man I think he is, it is not without the help of some god that he does all this. One of the immortals keeps near him, in a cloud of darkness, and turned back my arrow as it hit him. For I have let fly at him already and hit him clean through the breastplate on his right shoulder. I thought I had sent him off to Hades, but it seems not. Some god must be angry with me. And I am without my horses. I have eleven fair chariots with their horses at home. My father, that old spearman, said that I would need them. He was quite right, but I did not do what he said. I did not see how I would find enough food for them with all these others here. So I came on foot, and now my arrows have to let me down! I have hit two chiefs already, Diomede and Menelaus. I saw their blood clearly, but I have only made them angrier still. It was a bad day when I took down my curved bow and brought my

men here to Troy to please Hector. If ever I get back and
see my own country again and my wife and that great high-
roofed house of mine, may a stranger cut my head off then
and there if I do not break this bow with my own hands and
throw it into the fire. It is as much good to me as the wind."

Aeneas answered: "Do not talk like that. Things will not
get any better till we two drive against this man with chariot
and horses and take his measure in arms. Come and see what
these horses of mine are like, both for attacking and for
getting away. They will take us safely back to the city even
if Zeus gives Diomede the glory again. Will you take the
whip and reins while I do the fighting? Or will you take care
of him while I look after the horses?"

"You take the reins, Aeneas, and drive," said Pandarus.
"They are your own horses. They will do better with you
as charioteer, if we have to get away quickly. If they do
not hear your voice at the right time they may go stiff with
fear and let Diomede attack and kill us both and drive them
off himself. So you drive and I will keep my spear here
ready for him."

So they got up on the chariot and drove hard against Dio-
mede. Sthenelos, Diomede's driver, saw them and said to him:
"Here are two very strong fighters coming: Pandarus the
great bowman, and Aeneas whose mother was Aphrodite.
Come up in the chariot and let us move off. If you push too
far forward, you may get killed."

With an angry look Diomede answered him: "Do not
talk to me of running away. That sort of fight is not in
my blood. I am still full of strength. And I will not use

the chariot. I will face them on foot as I am. I am to fear no man, Pallas Athene said. Their swift horses will not take both these men out of the battle, even if one of them gets away. And note this. If Athene gives me this glory and I kill them both, hold onto your horses—give the reins a tight turn round the chariot rail—but spring upon Aeneas' horses and drive them away from the Trojans into the Greek army. For they are the best horses under the sun. They come from the horses Zeus gave to Tros for Ganymede."

By this time the others had driven up and Pandarus cried: "So my swift arrow did not kill you, great Diomede. Now let me see what my spear will do, if I can hit you."

And he threw and the far-shadowing spear hit Diomede's shield, and the bronze point cut through it and into his breastplate. Then loudly over him Pandarus gloried: "You are hit clean through the belly. Not for long will you live, and great is the glory you give me."

But with no touch of fear Diomede answered: "You have missed, not hit. And before the end of this, one or other of you two will have given up his blood in the dust to Ares."

He threw, and Athene guided the spear to Pandarus' nose near the eye, and it broke through his white teeth. The hard bronze cut through his tongue at its root and the point came out under his chin. He fell from the chariot, his bright-flashing armor ringing in his fall, and the swift-footed horses started for fear. There his life and strength were taken from him.

Then Aeneas jumped down with shield and spear, to keep the Greeks from dragging away the body. Lionlike in his strength he was, ready to kill whoever came at him and crying his terrible cry. But Diomede took up in his hand a stone—so great that two men, as men are now, could not have lifted it. And with this he hit Aeneas on the hip, where the leg turns in the hip joint, the "cup bone" its name is, and crushed it in, and the rough edge of the stone broke the skin open. Aeneas fell on his knees with one strong hand on the earth to hold him up. And the darkness of night covered his eyes.

Aeneas would have been killed then, but Aphrodite, his mother, saw. Quickly she came and put her arms round her dear son, and threw over him a fold of her white dress and was taking him out of the battle. But Diomede had seen that she was only Aphrodite, a feeble goddess not like Athene or Enyo, waster of cities. He came up with her and sprang at her and wounded her delicate skin with his sharp spear. It went right through her ambrosial dress to the inside of her forearm. Out came the immortal blood, the ichor, pouring from the wound. The gods do not eat bread or drink wine, so they have no such blood as ours. Aphrodite gave a loud cry and let her son fall, and Phoebus Apollo took him in his arms and saved him in a dark cloud. But Diomede, good at the war cry, shouted over Aphrodite: "Keep away, daughter of Zeus, from war and fighting. Let it be enough for you to trick feeble women. Come into battle and you will get what will make you shake all over at the very name of war."

The goddess ran from him and wind-footed Iris took her out of the battle to where Ares waited with his spear resting against a cloud and his two swift horses near. Aphrodite fell on her knees before her brother and prayed: "Dear brother, save me. Give me your horses to take me to Olympus. I am in pain, wounded by a mortal, Diomede, who is ready to fight now with father Zeus himself."

Ares gave her his horses and Iris got into the car with her and took the reins and whip. Quickly they came to high Olympus. There Iris unloosed them and put ambrosial food before them, while fair Aphrodite ran to her mother Dione's knees. She took her daughter in her arms and said: "Who of the sons of Heaven, dear child, has been so cruel to you, as though you had been doing something wrong?"

Laughter-loving Aphrodite answered: "Diomede, the high-hearted, wounded me because I was taking my dear son Aeneas, that I love best of all men, out of the battle. The war is no longer between the Trojans and Greeks, for the Greeks are fighting now even with the immortals."

"It is Athene," said Dione, "who put this foolish man, Diomede, on to this. Does he not know that he who fights with immortals does not live long, or hear his children about his knees when he comes back from the battle? Let Diomede take care; a better fighter than you may come against him. Then Aegialeia his brave wife will wake his house from its sleep, crying out for her husband."

So saying, with both hands she wiped the ichor from Aphrodite's arm, and the pain went away and the wound was well again. But Athene and Hera, looking on, had things to say they hoped would anger Zeus. "Aphrodite has been after some Greek woman," said Athene, "to get her to go with the Trojans she loves so much, and has got a scratch from one of the woman's pins."

But the father of gods and men smiled and said: "Aphrodite, you will never be a fighter. Keep to your own business and let Ares and Athene go to the wars."

So they talked. But Diomede sprang upon Aeneas, though he well knew that Apollo had him in his arms. He feared the great god not a bit, so great was his desire to kill Aeneas and take his glorious armor from him. Three times he sprang and three times Apollo threw him back. But when a fourth time he sprang at him like a god, Apollo, who sends his arrows far, shouted terribly at him. "Think, Diomede, and give way. Equal not your spirit with the gods. Men who walk the earth are not as the immortals."

Diomede then gave way a little space, while Apollo took Aeneas out of the battle to his temple in sacred Pergamos. There Leto and the archer Artemis made him well of his wound. But Apollo of the silver bow put a form like Aeneas, in armor like his, on the battlefield, and the Trojans and Greeks fought on over that.

Now Ares went down, in the form of Acamas, chief of the Thracians, and to Priam's sons he said: "How much longer will you let your army be killed off by the Greeks? Till they fight about our well-built gates? Aeneas is down, a man we honored even as much as Hector. Come, let us save his body out of the thick of the fighting."

With this he lifted up the strength and spirit of every man. And Sarpedon, son of Zeus, said bitter words to Hector. "Where is the strength you had before? You used to say,

Hector, that you and your brothers and brothers-in-law could hold the city by yourselves without any people or allies. But I do not see one of them here now. It is we, your allies only, who do the fighting. I come from far away, from Lycia and the banks of the river Xanthus. There my dear wife and young son are and my great wealth. Still I urge my Lycians on, and am ready myself to fight my man, though there is nothing of mine here for any Greek to take or drive off, while you simply stand about and do not even urge your men to fight to keep their wives safe. Look out or the Greeks will take your fair city before you know it."

So Sarpedon, son of Zeus, said and Hector's heart burned at his words. He sprang down from his chariot in his armor and waving his two spears high went everywhere urging his men to fight and shout the terrible war cry. So they came together and faced the Greeks again, but these stood firm against them. And Ares, to help the Trojans, covered them with a cloud of night and went everywhere among them to put courage in their hearts. He had seen Athene go and these were Apollo's orders. And Apollo himself sent Aeneas back into the fight full of courage to take his place in the battle. Great was the joy of the Trojans to see him living. But they could not question him, having other work to do.

On the other side the two Ajaxes and Odysseus and Diomede urged the Greeks on. But of themselves they stood unmoved; like mists which Zeus in still weather puts on the mountaintops when the North Wind and the other winds which blow the shadowy clouds about are sleeping, so unmoved stood the Greeks against the Trojan attack.

Then Hector ran upon them shouting loud and with him went Ares and dread Enyo, supporting Hector on every side.

Seeing him Diomede was shaken. Even as a man crossing a wide plain stops when he comes to a great river rolling on swiftly down to the sea—he sees its boiling waters and starts back in fear—so did Diomede give way. And to the Greeks he cried: "Friends, how can we wonder that Hector is such a spearman and fighter! Ever at his side is some god who keeps him safe from destruction. And now Ares is with him in the form of a mortal man. Keep your faces toward the Trojans but give way backward. We may not fight with gods."

In the middle of the battle Tlepolemus, son of Heracles, a brave man and tall, was moved by his fate to fight Sarpedon. As they came up against one another—the son and the grandson of the cloud-bringer, Zeus—Tlepolemus cried: "Sarpedon, counselor of the Lycians, what are you doing here, a man who knows nothing of war? Why do they falsely say you are a son of Zeus? Very different you are from his sons in the days of old. Far other was Heracles, the lionhearted, my own brave father, who came here with six ships only and a handful of men and still took the city of Troy and made waste her streets. But yours is a coward's heart and your people are falling away from you. No help to the Trojans will your coming be, however strong you are, but through the gates of Hades will you go sent by my hand."

Sarpedon, chief of the Lycians, answered: "Tlepolemus,

it is true that your father took sacred Troy, because lordly Laomedon, whom he had served so well, gave him hard words in place of the horses for which he had come so far. But you, I think, will get death here at my hands, and give glory to me and your soul to Hades—who has good horses, too."

Tlepolemus lifted his arm and they threw their long spears together. Sarpedon hit him full on the neck, and the point went right through, and dark night came down upon his eyes. But Tlepolemus hit Sarpedon in the left thigh and the point scratched the bone; but for the present his father, Zeus, kept Sarpedon from destruction.

The Lycians took Sarpedon out of the battle, the long spear pulling at him cruelly as it dragged. But no man saw it or thought of taking it out to let him stand on his feet. Such bad work they made of caring for him.

The Greeks, too, took Tlepolemus away. Odysseus saw and his heart was moved to take the lives of the Lycians. Eight of them he killed and would have killed more but great Hector of the flashing helm saw and came, bringing fear to the Greeks. Sarpedon was glad at his coming and cried: "Son of Priam, let me not rest here to fall into the hands of the Greeks, but help me. Let me die in your city, if I am not to go back home to my own country and make my dear wife and child glad again."

But Hector had no word for him in answer. He ran by, so much he desired to drive the Greeks back and take the lives of many. Then his friends put Sarpedon under a fair oak, the tree of Zeus, and from his thigh they pushed the spear. His spirit gave up and a mist fell over his eyes. Presently he came to himself again, for the breath of the North Wind as it played upon him made him live again after he had breathed out his spirit.

When the goddess, white-armed Hera, saw what Hector and Ares were doing, she said to Athene: "Was it for this we gave our word to Menelaus that he would not come home again till he had taken Troy? Let us go into the battle." Then she made ready her flaming chariot while Athene armed herself for the fight. The two drove out through the gates of Heaven, which the Hours had in their keeping in whose care are great Heaven and Olympus, to throw open the thick cloud or shut it to. Through the gate they drove their horses and found the son of Cronos seated away from the other gods on the topmost point of Olympus. And white-armed Hera questioned all-highest Zeus. "Father Zeus, are you not angry with Ares for these highhanded doings? See how many of the Greeks he has killed to my sorrow, and with no right or reason, while Aphrodite and Apollo are looking on at it all with pleasure. They put this madman to work. Father Zeus, will you be angry with me if I hit Ares hard and drive him out of the battle?"

And Zeus, bringer of clouds, answered: "Why do you not get Athene to go for him? She punishes him more frequently than any of you others." And Hera took note of his word. They went down to the land of Troy where the two rivers, the Simoïs and Scamander, join their waters. There Hera loosed her horses and put thick mist about them; and Simoïs made ambrosia spring up for them to eat.

Then the goddesses went to where the bravest stood about great Diomede, and Hera put on the form of bronze-voiced Stentor, whose cry is as loud as the voice of fifty men, and shouted: "Shame on you cowardly Greeks, brave only in looks. When Achilles was fighting, the Trojans would never come even out before the Dardanian gate, such was their dread of his spear. But now they are fighting at the hollow ships far from the city."

With this she put strength and spirit into them all. And Athene went up to Diomede. He was airing the wound Pandarus gave him with the arrow. For the sweat caused by the band that took the weight of his shield was making it worse. His arm was stiff and tired with the pain and he was lifting up this band to wipe away the blood. The goddess put her hand on his chariot rail and said: "Your father Tydeus was very different. He was a little man but he could fight, even when I told him not to. When he went by himself to the city of Thebes among the Cadmeians, I told him to feast in their houses in peace. But with that high spirit he always had, he stood up against all their young men and overcame them in everything, so much I helped him. But as for you, I help you in every way, too, and I tell you to fight the Trojans; but either you are tired out or afraid of them. You are no true son of Tydeus."

Then great Diomede answered: "I know you, goddess, and I will tell you how it is. I am not afraid, or downhearted, but I am keeping in mind the orders you gave me. You told me not to fight face to face with any of the gods. Only if Aphrodite came into the battle, I was to wound her with my spear. That is why I am giving way here, and telling all the rest of the Greeks to do the same, because I see Ares there helping Hector."

"Diomede, son of Tydeus," said Athene, "man after my own heart, do not be afraid now of Ares or any other of the immortals, so much will I help you. Drive your horses straight at Ares now and wound him. Have no fear of this madman who fights first on one side then on the other. He was talking with Hera and me and saying he would help the Greeks against the Trojans. And now he has gone over to the Trojans."

So saying she pushed Sthenelos out of the chariot with her hand and he jumped down. And she stepped up into it at Diomede's side, a goddess burning for battle, and took the reins and whip and drove straight at Ares. He was taking the armor off tall Periphas, the best of the Aetolians. And Athene put on the headdress of Hades, so that Ares could not see her.

When Ares saw Diomede, he let Periphas be and made straight for Diomede. When they came near, Ares threw his spear first, but the goddess waved it up with her hand to fly over their heads. Then Diomede threw; and Athene guided the spear to the lowest part of Ares' belly; and Ares cried out as loudly as nine or ten thousand fighting men can shout. The Greeks and the Trojans all shook with fear, so loudly was Ares, tireless of war, crying out.

As a black undercloud in the sky when sudden winds come up after great heat, so Ares seemed to Diomede as he went up into wide Heaven. Quickly he came to high

Olympus to the house of the gods, and in great pain sat down by the side of Zeus pointing to the immortal blood pouring from the wound and he cried: "Father Zeus, are you not angry? We gods are cruel to one another, though kind to men. That mad daughter of yours, always thinking of some evil to do, puts all of us against you. We all do as you tell us; but she need not. You do not care what she does, but back her because she is your daughter. Now she has made Diomede turn his spear even on the immortal gods. First it was Aphrodite he wounded, and then he sprang on me as though he were a god. My swift feet had to take me away quickly or I would have lived on without my strength through what his spear would have done."

Then with an angry look Zeus, the cloud-bringer, answered: "Do not come crying here, you double-faced turncoat. I hate you more than any other god on Olympus. You love nothing but wars and fighting. You have the impossible spirit of your mother Hera. It is hard enough to keep her in control whatever I say. And this trouble of yours is her doing. However, I can't let you go on in such pain. You are my son, after all. But if you had been the son of some other god, by this time you would have been down lower than the Titans, the sons of Heaven."

And he told Paeëon to make the wound well. And Paeëon put pain-killing leaves upon it, and he was well again. And Hebe washed him and clothed him and he took his seat by his father Zeus, full of joy in his glory.

But Hera and Athene, now that they had put a stop to Ares' killings, went back again to the house of Zeus.

6

SO THE war was left to itself, and to this side and to that they fought over the plain, between the waters of Simoïs and Xanthus. And many were killed on both sides.

But Menelaus took Adrastus alive. Adrastus' horses ran into a tree as they were flying madly across the plain and the chariot was broken. The horses went off toward the city, but Adrastus rolled out from the chariot and fell by the wheel in the dust on his face. To him came Menelaus, with his far-shadowing spear in his hands. Adrastus took him by the knees and prayed for his life: "Take me alive, son of Atreus; many treasures of bronze and gold and iron are stored in my father's house. My father will give you more than can be measured if he hears that I am alive at the Greek ships."

Menelaus was ready to have him taken to the ships, but Agamemnon came running up to him and said: "Why be softhearted, Menelaus? Have the Trojans been so kind to you in your house? Let not one of them get away from us alive, not even a man-child of them in his mother's womb. Let them all die together, uncared for and unknown."

And he turned his brother's mind. So Menelaus pushed Adrastus from him and Agamemnon hit him as he fell over, and then planted his heel on his chest and pulled out the spear.

Then Nestor cried to the Greeks: "Friends, fighters, servants of Ares, let no man now wait to take their armor from the dead, to go back to the ships with the greatest store. Kill the men. Later, you can take their armor from them in peace, as you will."

With this, he lifted the strength and spirit of every man, and the Greeks would have driven the Trojans to Troy, if Helenus, the seer, son of Priam, had not come to Aeneas and Hector, to say: "On you more than any, the weight of the war rests, for you are the first in all things, in counsel and in fighting. Now hold firm, go everywhere through the army and keep their hearts up before the gates or they will go running in to their women's arms and great will be the joy of the Greeks. When you have put new heart into them, we will fight on here, tired though we are; but you, Hector, must go into the city and tell our mother to bring all the chief women to Athene's temple in the city, and open the doors of the sacred house, and put the best and fairest dress she has, the one she herself cares most for, on the knees of the goddess, and swear an offering of twelve smooth-haired undriven cattle, if she will have pity on the wives and little children of the Trojans, and keep back from sacred Troy this Diomede, the great spearman, who now seems truly the best of the Greeks. We did not fear even Achilles so much, born of a goddess, though he is, men say. This man rages out of all measure, and no one is his equal in strength."

And Hector did as his brother said. He went through all the army and gave them new heart, till they turned again with their faces toward the Greeks. And these thought that some one of the immortals had come down from starry Heaven to help the Trojans, so strangely was their strength increased. And Hector shouted loud to the Trojans: "High-hearted Trojans and allies, be men, my friends, and full of courage, while I go to Troy to tell the old men, the counselors, and our wives to pray and make offerings to the gods."

So saying Hector of the flashing helmet turned to the city and the black skin edge of his shield touched his feet and neck as he went his way.

Now Glaucus, son of Hippolochus, and Diomede came together between the two armies to fight together. And Diomede cried: "Who are you among men? I have not seen you till now. Bravest of all you must be to come forward so to meet my far-shadowing spear. If you are one of the immortal gods, I will not fight you. They do not live long who fight against the gods. But if you are of men who eat the fruit of the earth, come near and meet your end."

Then Glaucus said: "Great-souled son of Tydeus, why do you ask who I am? Men come and go as the leaves do on the trees. In the fall, the wind takes off the leaves and to the earth they go, but in the spring the trees put out new growth. So, too, with men; one goes and another comes. But, if you will, these are my forefathers' names; they are known to many. There is a city, Ephyre, in the heart of Argos, where lived Sisyphus, most designing of men. His son Glaucus was the father of Bellerophon, the unequaled. Beautiful and fair to look upon, the gods made him. But Proetus designed evil against him and being the stronger drove him from the Argive lands over which Zeus had made him ruler. For Anteia, the wife of Proetus, would have had Bellerophon lie with her in love secretly. But he would not, for his heart was upright. So she said falsely to King Proetus: 'Either die yourself, Proetus, or kill Bellerophon, because he desired to lie with me against my will.' The king was angered, but would not kill him—his soul had fear of that. So he sent him to Lycia and gave him deadly signs cut in a secret tablet and told him to give them to Anteia's father who, seeing them, would kill him. So Bellerophon went to Lycia and the gods took him there safely. For nine days the king of wide Lycia did him honor. But when rose-fingered Dawn came for the tenth time, he asked to see the tablet. After seeing it he ordered Bellerophon first to kill the raging Chimaera. She was of the gods, not of men, in front a lion, in the middle a goat with the tail of a snake and she breathed out flaming fire. But Bellerophon killed her by the help of the gods. Then he fought with the Solymi —the greatest of all his battles he said—and thirdly he killed the Amazons, women the equals of men. But as he journeyed back, the king sent the bravest men in all wide Lycia to kill him. Not a man of these came home, for Bellerophon killed them all. Then the king knew that he was the brave offspring of a god, so he gave him his own daughter as wife and made him equal with himself in honor. And there were born to wise-hearted Bellerophon three children: Isander and Hippolochus and Laodameia. Zeus, the counselor, lay with Laodameia and her son is godlike Sarpedon. But even Bellerophon came to be hated by the gods, and he journeyed alone, eating his own heart, far from men, all over the Aleian plain. Isander his son was killed warring against the Solymi, and his daughter was killed by Artemis in anger. But Hippolochus was my father and he sent me to Troy, telling me to be the bravest of all and not to shame the blood of my fathers, who were the noblest by far in Ephyre and in wide Lycia. This is the blood of which I come."

So he said, and Diomede was glad. He planted his spear in the fruitful earth and answered him with friendly words: "Truly then you are an old friend of my father's house. Great Oeneus of old feasted Bellerophon there for twenty days. And they gave one another fair gifts. I have Bellerophon's great gold cup at home. I have no memory of Tydeus myself for I was only a little child when he went away with the Greek army to die at Thebes. But you and I must be friends now. I will take care of you in Argos and you of me in Lycia, if ever I go there. So let us keep away from one another's spears here. There are enough Trojans and noble allies for me to kill, if a god lets me and my feet can over-take them; and many Greeks for you to kill if you can. And let us exchange armor, as a sign to all that we are old friends from our fathers' days."

With these words they sprang from their chariots and swore to be friends, hand held in hand. Then Zeus, son of Cronos, took his senses away from Glaucus, for he ex-changed golden armor for bronze, the value of a hundred oxen for the value of nine.

When Hector came to the Scaean gate and the oak tree, the wives and daughters of the Trojans came running round him to ask about their sons and brothers and friends and husbands. And he ordered them all to pray in turn to the gods, but sorrows were hanging over many.

He went on to the house of Priam the King—where were fifty bedrooms of polished stone for Priam's sons and their wives. And Hecuba, Hector's mother, met him and she of-fered him wine, but he said: "Bring me no honey-hearted wine, honored mother, or you may un-man me and put what I have to do out of my mind. And with unwashed hands, dirty with blood, I would fear to make drink offer-ings to Zeus. No, go and pray to Athene so that she may take pity on Troy and the Trojans." And he told her what Helenus had said. And Hecuba went to the treas-ure room, where her richly worked dresses lay, the handi-work of Sidonian women, whom Paris had brought with him from Sidon as he sailed over the wide sea when he brought back high-born Helen. And she took the fairest of her dresses, bright like a star it was, that lay under all the others. And she gave it to the priestess of Athene, who put it on Athene's knees. And Hecuba prayed Athene to break Diomede's spear, and have pity on the Trojans. But Athene would not.

Hector went his way to the house of Paris and he found him there playing with his beautiful armor and near him Helen sat among her women overlooking their handiwork. When he saw Paris, Hector cried: "What has come over you, Paris? What have you against the Trojans in your heart? The people die before the walls and war flames round the city because of you. You would be angry yourself to see another man hanging back from the fight. Up, quickly, or the city will be burnt."

And Paris answered: "You are right, Hector. But it is nothing against the Trojans, only sorrow at heart, that has kept me back. Helen here, even now, was telling me to fight. And I think, myself, it will be better so. We may win still. Wait while I arm, or go ahead. I will overtake you."

Hector did not answer, but Helen said to him softly: "O brother! Dog that I am, troublemaker, hated by all. Would that the storm wind had taken me away on the day my mother bore me—had taken me away to some mountain or far out to sea where the loud waves would have gone over me—before all these things came to be. But seeing that the gods designed all this, would that I had been wife to a better man. This man's mind is never fixed nor ever will be, and now the fruit of it all is coming to him. But sit and rest yourself here, Hector. Yours is the greatest care—all because of shameless me and the sin of Paris. Zeus brings an evil fate on us, so that we may be a song in the ears of future men."

But Hector answered: "Do not tell me to sit, Helen, if you love me. I must go back to help the Trojans. Send this man quickly after me to overtake me while I am in the city. I am going by my house to see my wife and son, for I do not know if the gods will kill me at the hands of the Greeks, or let me come home again."

So Hector of the bright helm went to his house but he did not find his wife Andromache there; and he asked her women and they told him: "She heard the Trojans were in great danger, so like one out of her mind she went to look out from the high wall of Troy."

Then quickly Hector went down through the streets by the way he had come. When he came to the Scaean gates and was going out onto the plain, Andromache came running and after her came a nurse with Hector's baby son in her arms—beautiful he was as a star. Hector had named him Scamandrius, but the people Astyanax—King of the city—for only Hector guarded Troy. Hector smiled as he looked on the boy in silence and Andromache took his hands in her own with tears in her eyes.

"Strange man," she said, "your courage will be your destruction. You have no pity for me or for your little son. As for me, if you fall, it would be better for me to be dead. For I have no father or mother. Achilles killed my father, Eëtion, but he did not take his armor—he had too much pity and fear to do that. He gave him to the fire and built a mound over him. And my seven brothers he killed on the same day among their cattle and white-wooled sheep. My mother he freed for a great price, but Artemis the archer queen killed her in her father's house. No, Hector, you are father and mother and brother and dear husband to me. Have pity on us. Stay here on the wall. Do not make your son fatherless. Bring the army back to the fig tree, where the wall, as the Greeks know, is most open to attack."

And Hector answered: "Wife, I too have thought of this, but how could I face the Trojans, or their wives, if I kept out of the battle now? I cannot do it, now that I have learned to be brave and fight always at the head of the Trojans to win glory for my father and myself. I know well that the day is coming when Troy and Priam and Priam's people must go down before the Greeks; but for none of these do I sorrow as for you when some bronze-coated Greek takes you away—to work at the loom in Argos, maybe, or bring water from the spring under some cruel master. May I be dead and earth cover me before that."

And he stretched out his arms to his son, but the little boy turned away in fear of the great bronze helmet and the crest of horsehair waving down upon him. Then Hector and Andromache laughed at him together and Hector took off his helmet and put it down. And he took his son and kissed him and prayed. "Zeus and all you other gods, may this boy be as I am, as strong and as brave, and rule over Troy. And may some day some man say of him as he comes in from the fighting: 'He is better far than his father,' and may his mother then be happy in her heart."

And he gave the boy back to his dear wife and she took him to her breast, smiling through her tears. And she went back to the house of man-killing Hector and there she and her women sorrowed loud for Hector while he was still alive, for they thought that never again would he come back from battle, safe from the hands of the Greeks.

Paris was not long in coming. He put on his glorious armor and ran down through the city. As a horse that has had his full feed of grain breaks loose and runs swiftly all over the plain, holding his head high in his joy and pride, and his knees take him lightly to where the mares are feeding, so Paris, son of Priam, ran down from high Pergamus, flashing in his armor like the sun, laughing for pleasure, and his swift feet took him on. Quickly he overtook his brother and said: "I have kept you waiting, Hector. I did not come as quickly as you told me."

And Hector answered: "What now! No one in his right mind can think little of your work in battle; but you do not take things seriously. You don't care. That is why it is so bad when the Trojans say what they do about you. You are the cause of all their troubles. But let us go on our way. We will look into all this later, if Zeus ever lets us hold out the cup of thank-offering in our houses, after we have driven the Greeks out of the land of Troy."

7

H ECTOR, and Paris with him, went swiftly out
through the gates, both high in heart. And as
when a god sends a fair wind to seamen who are
tired out with pulling their polished oars of fir, so
their coming seemed to the Trojans. Then they and Glaucus
killed many.

But when Athene saw what they were doing, she came
down from Olympus. And Apollo went out from Pergamus
and they met by the oak tree. Then the two of them moved
the Greeks and Trojans to put an end to their fighting for
the day.

When the Greeks were back at their ships, they feasted

and held counsel. And it seemed best to them, counseled by Nestor, to build a high wall with a deep ditch before it, full of sharp-pointed stakes, as a defense to their ships. And to put gates in the wall so that chariots could come through.

And in Troy, too, they held counsel. And at dawn they sent Idaeus, the herald, to the Greeks to tell Agamemnon and Menelaus that Paris would give back the treasure he took with Helen, but not Helen herself.

When the Greeks heard him, all were silent till Diomede said: "Let no man now take this treasure from Paris; no, nor Helen herself. For it is clear now, even to a man out of his mind, how near the Trojans are to their fate." And all shouted that he was right. But Trojans and Greeks agreed to have peace for the day while they burned the bodies of the dead. And they did so; and the Greeks built their wall.

And when it was done, ships came to the Greeks from Lemnos bringing wine. And from these the long-haired Greeks bought wine, some with bronze, some with iron, some with skins, some with whole cattle and some with slaves; and the whole night through they feasted. And in the city, the Trojans and their allies feasted, too. But all night long Zeus, the counselor, thundered terribly. Fear took hold of them and they let the wine drop from their cups on the ground. And no man would drink till he had made drink offerings to the son of Cronos, powerful over all. Then they lay down and took the gift of sleep.

8

DAWN was coming over the face of all the earth when Zeus, who throws the thunderbolt, brought the gods together in council on the topmost point of Olympus and said: "Hear me, all you gods and goddesses, and the word I have in mind to say. Make no attempt, any of you, against it; I will bring all this now to an end. If I see any of you helping either the Trojans or the Greeks, I will take and throw him far down into dark Tartarus, iron gated and bronze floored, as far down under Hades as Heaven is high over the earth. Then you may learn how much my power is greater than yours."

They were all silent, but after a time Athene said: "Father of all of us, son of Cronos, highest of all, we know well that no one can stand against your will. But even so, we have pity upon the Greek spearmen, who are now to be killed. We will keep away from the battle, as you say, but we will give them counsel which may be some profit to them, so that they do not all die through your anger."

With a smile, Zeus answered: "Take heart, my child. I am not as serious as I seem."

So saying he went in his chariot to many-springed Ida, to Gargarus where his sweet-smelling altar is. There he loosed his horses and put thick mist round them and took his seat, full of joy in his glory, looking down on the city of the Trojans and the ships of the Greeks.

Then the two armies were joined in battle.

Now all morning long as the sacred day increased, so long the spears and arrows hit hard and men kept falling. But when the sun came to middle Heaven, the Father lifted high his golden balance; and in them he put two fates of death, one for the horse-taming Trojans and one for the bronze-coated Greeks; he held the balance by the middle and lifted it up, and the fate of the Greeks went down. Then Zeus thundered loud from Ida, sending a bolt among the Greeks, and seeing it they wondered and were afraid.

And Hector shouted loud: "Trojans and Lycians and Dardanians, take heart. I see that Zeus now gives glory to us and destruction to the Greeks. They were fools to build this wall. Our horses will lightly spring across that ditch. But when I come to their ships, see that you bring me fire to burn them, while I kill the Greeks by their ships in the smoke."

And he cried to his horses. "Xanthus and Podargus, Aethon and Lampus, pay me for your keep now, and for all the honey-sweet grain which Andromache has given you, and for the wine and water she mixed for you—even before giving me, her husband, any."

Now all the space inside the wall was full of chariots and men, all herded there together by Hector, now that the hand of Zeus was with him. And he would have burned the fair ships then with flaming fire, but Hera put it in Agamemnon's mind to lift up the hearts of the Greeks. He went his way by the ships and took his stand by Odysseus' black ship in the middle where a shout could be heard from both ends, from the huts of Ajax to those of Achilles, for these two, knowing their own courage and the strength of their hands, had put their ships at the ends of the line. Then he shouted: "Shame on you Greeks, good-lookers only. At Lemnos you said at the feast that each one of you could face a hundred, two hundred Trojans. Now we cannot even face one, this Hector, who will quickly burn our ships with flaming fire. Father Zeus, was there ever another king whose soul you blinded like this, to take this great glory from him?" And Father Zeus had pity on his tears.

But to Hera he said: "At dawn if you will, O ox-eyed, queenly Hera, you may see me working even worse evil on the Greek spearmen. For dread Hector will not turn back till swift-footed Achilles takes up his arms again, when they are fighting by the ships' sterns over Patroclus' body. Such is the word of Heaven."

So he said and Hera made no answer. Then into Oceanus fell the sun and black night came over earth, the grain giver. Against their will the Trojans saw the daylight going; but welcome, and three times prayed for, was dark night to the Greeks.

Then Hector took the Trojans back from the ships to a space by the riverside that was clear of dead bodies. There he stood among them holding a sixteen-foot spear in his hand with a ring of gold round its bronze spear point. And he said to them: "I thought we would have burned the ships and killed all the Greeks before we went back again to Troy. But night came on too early and saved them. So now let us give in to the dark and make supper ready. Loose the horses and give them their feed. Bring oxen and sheep from the city, with honey-hearted wine and bread from your houses, and enough wood to make good fires all night through. We need their light to see what the Greeks are doing. I do not want any of them to get away safe to sea. Let heralds cry in the city that all old men and young boys are to man the walls, and let the women build great fires, and keep a good watch, so that no force can get into the city. I pray in high hope to Zeus to drive out these dogs sent here by the fates. And we will guard ourselves here; but, in the morning, to battle at the hollow ships. I would that I might be immortal, honored as Athene and Apollo, as certainly as tomorrow brings evil on the Greeks."

So he said and all the Trojans shouted loudly. And quickly

they got their oxen and sheep, and their honey-hearted wine and bread from their houses, and the wood and made their offerings to the immortals. The winds took the sweet smell from the plain up into Heaven. But the gods took no pleasure in it, for they bitterly hated Troy and Priam and Priam's people.

With high hearts they rested there the whole night through among their watch fires. Even as when in Heaven the stars are clear above and the bright moon, and no wind moves, and all the mountains and high headlands stand out, and from Heaven breaks open the limitless air and all the stars are seen and the shepherd has joy in his heart—so between the ships and the waters of Xanthus were the watch fires of the Trojans before Troy. Fifty men sat by each watch fire. And their horses, eating their feed, stood by the chariots and waited for Dawn.

9

BUT IN the Greek camp the chiefs, sad hearted, sat together in the place of meeting. And Agamemnon stood up before them in tears—like dark water that runs down over the face of a cliff were his tears—and with deep moans he said: "My friends, chiefs and rulers of the Greeks: cruel Zeus, though he said before that Troy would be ours, now sends us home in dishonor. This is his pleasure and his power is over all. So now let us take to our ships and go home to our own country; for we may hope no more to take wide-streeted, high-walled Troy."

They sat there saying nothing for a long time, till Diomede of the loud war cry answered: "Son of Atreus, what has come upon you now, to think we are all as feeble and unwarlike as you say? Go if you will; the way is open before you. There are your ships lined up on the sand, the many ships which came here with you. We others of the long-haired Greeks will stay here till we have wasted Troy. Or if the rest will go with you, let them! Sthenelos and I, at least, will fight on till we have taken Troy, for with the help of Heaven we came."

Then all the Greeks cried out for Diomede and Nestor stood up, the oldest of them all, the clear-voiced old counselor. He said: "I, who am older than you, will make all clear and no man, no, not even chief Agamemnon, will take my words lightly. But first let us give way to black night and make ready our supper."

So Agamemnon took the Greek chiefs to his hut and gave them there a feast to do good to their hearts. And when they had put from them the desire for food and drink, Nestor went on: "Agamemnon, chief of chiefs, Zeus has given rule and judgment to you, and it is for you to do what may seem best for us all. So I will say what I have had in mind from the day when you took the girl, Briseis, from angry Achilles' hut. Against our will you did it, when your high heart made you put dishonor on a man honored by the very gods. But now let us take thought how we may win him back—with what gifts and with what words."

And Agamemnon answered: "Old sir, what you say is in no way wrong. I was blind. A man Zeus loves in his heart, as he loves this man Achilles, is more than an army; and the Greeks die for it. So, because I was blind and let my anger rule me, I am ready now to give great gifts to get him back. Let me name them before you all: seven tripods untouched by the fire, and ten talents of gold and twenty bright cauldrons, and twelve strong horses, swift to win prizes. And with them I will give seven women, clever workers and very beautiful—women I selected on the day when Achilles himself took well-built Lesbos. I will give him all these and with them Briseis whom I took away that day. And I will swear a great oath that I never came near her bed or touched her in the way of man and woman. All this now. And as to the future, if the gods let us take Troy, he may put all the gold and bronze he desires in his hollow ship and select twenty women—the most beautiful there are after Argive Helen. And if we come back safely to Argos, let him be my son and I will honor him like Orestes. Of my three daughters let him take which one he will to his father's house in marriage and I will add greater gifts than any man ever before gave with his daughter. For I will give him seven cities—near the sea they all are, on the edge of sandy Pylos, and they who live there are rich in sheep and cattle. They will honor him with gifts as though he were a god and be happy under his rule. All this is if Achilles will put an end to his anger. Let him give way—only Hades will never give way; that is why he is to mortals the most hated of all the gods. Let Achilles change his mind. I am a greater chief than he is and an older man."

Then answered old Nestor: "Most great Agamemnon, these truly are gifts which no man may look down on. Who are the best men to go to Achilles' hut? Send these: old

Phoenix first, to go ahead, and then Ajax and Odysseus, and two heralds with them. And now with clean hands let us keep a sacred silence while we make our prayer to Zeus, may he have pity upon us."

His words pleased them all. Then the heralds gave them water for their hands to wash them and the young men gave them full wine cups for their drink offerings. And after drinking what they desired, Phoenix, Ajax, and Odysseus went their way by the edge of the loud-sounding sea with many a prayer that Achilles' heart might be changed. And they came to the huts of the Myrmidons and there he was, playing on a silver-bridged lyre he had taken from Eëtion's city. He was singing of heroes, and Patroclus sat over against him in silence, waiting for the end of his song.

They came forward, Odysseus first, and stood before him. And Achilles jumped up in surprise when he saw them —keeping the lyre in his hand. Then he said: "Welcome. Truly you are friends who come. Great must be the need. Even in my anger you are the dearest to me of the Greeks." So saying, he took them into his hut and seated them on beds covered with purple, and to Patroclus he cried: "Get a deeper bowl and mix less water in the wine and give a cup to each man, for these are my best friends who are under my roof."

And Patroclus did so, and he put a great wood block to cut on in the light of the fire and on it a sheep's back and a goat's, and the back of a pig rich with fat. And Achilles cut up the meat and put it upon thin sticks, and Patroclus made the fire burn up brightly. When it burned down he put the meat, with sacred salt upon it, over the coals. And when it was ready Achilles served it while Patroclus put bread on the table in fair baskets. Then Achilles sat down facing Odysseus and ordered Patroclus to make a burnt offering and Patroclus did so. Then they took of the good things before them. And when they had put from them the desire of food and drink, Ajax made a sign to Phoenix. But Odysseus saw it, took up his cup of wine, drank to Achilles and said: "Hail, O Achilles! We are not short of the equal feast either in Agamemnon's hut or here in yours. But other things than feasts are now in our thoughts, for we see destruction near. We fear we will not be able to save the ships if you will not take up your arms again to help us. The watch fires of the Trojans—many as the stars—are round our camp. Zeus has given them signs, lightning on their right; and Hector, high in heart—taking Zeus for his helper —cares not for men or gods, in his madness. His prayer is: 'Come quickly, sacred Dawn, that I may burn the ships and kill the Greeks in the thick of their smoke!' This is our fear. Will the gods let him do it? Is it our fate to die here before Troy? Up then, even at this last hour, if you have a mind to save us! Sorrow will come to you later if you will not; what is done cannot be undone; think now how you can save the Greeks, before it is too late. Did not your father, Peleus, say to you, when he sent you to Agamemnon from Phthia: 'My son, Athene and Hera will make you strong, if they are so minded; but do you keep down your pride, for goodwill is better; so may the Greeks, old and young, honor you the more'. These were the old man's words; you have not kept them in mind. But give way now and put your bitter anger from you.

"Agamemnon offers you great enough gifts, if you will. These namely: seven tripods untouched by the fire, and ten talents of gold and twenty bright cauldrons, and twelve strong horses, swift to win prizes. And with them seven women, clever workers and very beautiful. He will give you all these and with them Briseis. And he will swear a great oath that he never came near her bed or touched her in the way of man and woman. All this now. And in days to come, if the gods let us take Troy, you may put all the gold and bronze you desire in your hollow ship and select twenty women—the most beautiful there are after Argive Helen. And if we come back safely to Argos, you may be his son and he will honor you like Orestes. Of his three daughters you may take which one you will to your father's house in marriage and he will add greater gifts than any man ever before gave with his daughter. For he will give you seven cities—near the sea they all are, on the edge of sandy Pylos, and those who live there are rich in sheep and cattle. And they will honor you with gifts as though you were a god and be happy under your rule. All this is if you will put an end to your anger.

"But if you hate Agamemnon and his gifts too deeply, then at least have pity on the rest of us. And you could kill Hector. He will come very near you now in his rage. He thinks there is no man equal to him among all the Greeks who came in their ships to Troyland."

Then swift-footed Achilles answered: "Zeus-born son of

Laërtes, man of many designings, now I must say what I have in mind and what I will do, so that you may not sit before me and argue this way and that. I hate—like the gates of Hades—a man who says one thing and has another in his heart. Agamemnon and the other Greeks will not win me over. For, it seems, there is to be no thanks for all our endless fighting. The man who stays at home gets as much as the man who fights his best. The fearful and the fearless are equally honored. Death comes to the do-nothing and to the hard worker alike. What profit have I had from all that I have gone through and all the dangers of these wars? Like a mother bird who gives everything she can get to her little ones and herself goes without, so I have watched out many a sleepless night before many a bloody day of battle, fighting against people who were only fighting to keep their women safe. Twelve towns I have wasted from shipboard and eleven from land, I would have you know, throughout fertile Troyland, and what I took from them, and no little it was, I gave to Agamemnon and he, who had stayed at home among the ships, would divide some small part but keep the most. Some he gave as prizes of honor to the chiefs and kings and they have them now. Only from me of all the Greeks did he take a prize, my wife—let him sleep by her side and take his joy! But why must the Greeks make war on the Trojans? Why has Agamemnon brought all these fighters here? Because of fair-haired Helen? Are Agamemnon and Menelaus the only ones who love their wives? Does not every man in his right mind love his dear one—as I loved mine with all my heart, even though I took her with my spear? But now that he has taken away my prize of honor, he cannot trick me again. I know him too well. No, Odysseus, let him work out with you and the other chiefs how to save the ships from burning. See how much he has done already without my help. He has built a wall and made a ditch and put sharp stakes in it. But even all this somehow does not keep Hector back. When I was in the field Hector did not go very far from Troy—no farther than the Scaean gates and the oak tree. He did wait once for me there by himself and only got away from me with some trouble. But now I have no mind to fight with Hector, so tomorrow, if you care to, you may see my ships sailing at daybreak over Hellespont; and, if the great Earthshaker is kind, I will be back on the third day in deep-soiled Phthia with all my goods again. Only from me has a prize of honor been taken by him that gave it, even Agamemnon. Tell him what I say, every word, and publicly, so that the other Greeks may see him for what he is. I will have nothing to do with him. Let him go his way to destruction; Zeus has taken away his reason. As for his gifts, even if he gave me ten or twenty times as much, all he has or all he ever may have—gifts as many as the sands of the sea or the dust of the earth—I will not be moved till he has paid in full for the bitter wrong he has done me. And I will not take his daughter, not if she were as beautiful as golden Aphrodite herself and matched in handiwork bright-eyed Athene. No, let him give her to another, to some man like himself and more of a king than I am! If the gods keep me and send me back safe to my home, my father Peleus himself will find me a wife. There are many women in Hellas and Phthia, daughters of kings, and one of these I will make my dear wife. Many a time I have been minded to take a wife and live at home with all the good things which my father Peleus has there. For my life is more to me than even all the riches men say that Troy, the well-peopled city, had of old in the days of peace before ever the Greeks came to Troyland, or than all the gold on the stone floor of Apollo's temple under the cliffs of Pytho. Oxen and sheep a man may get with the spear, and tripods and horses, too, may be won; but when a man's life has once gone from between his teeth, nothing we can do will bring it back. My goddess mother, silver-footed Thetis, has told me that twofold fates are taking me forward to death. If I stay here warring about Troy, there will be no home-coming for me, though my name will live forever. But if I go back to my dear homeland, my name will die, though it will be long before death takes me. And to you other Greeks I would say, Sail home, too. You will never take Troy, for the hand of Zeus is over her. So go back to the chiefs and tell them to find some other way of saving their ships. But let Phoenix stay here and sleep, and sail with me tomorrow, if he will. I will not take him by force."

They sat there in silence, for very violently had he said "No." At last the old man Phoenix, bursting into tears, so much he feared for the Greek ships, said to him: "O great Achilles, if this is your mind, how can I stay here without you? Your father Peleus ordered me to be with you when he sent you to Agamemnon; a boy only you were then, who

knew nothing of war or of the meetings where men make
their mark. I was to teach you all this—how to say what
must be said and do what must be done. I will not stay here
without you, not though a god took my old age off me and
made me as strong as I was when I ran away from my fa-
ther. He was very angry with me because of his fair-haired
concubine. He loved her and thought nothing of my mother.
So my mother prayed me by my knees to make love to the
woman myself and make her hate my father. But he came to
know and put a curse upon me, crying on the dread Erinyes
to witness, that no son of mine might ever sit on my knees,
and the gods, Zeus of the under earth and dread Persephone,
made his word come true. I had it in my heart to kill him, but
some god held my hand, bringing to my mind what the
Greeks say of a man who kills his father. So I ran away from
my father's house and came to deep-soiled Phthia and king
Peleus was kind to me and made me ruler over the Dolo-
pians. And I brought you up to be what you are, O godlike
Achilles, loving you from my heart, for never would you go
to the feast or touch meat till I took you on my knees and cut
up your food and put the wine cup to your lips. How many
times have you wetted my shirt slobbering out your wine,
helpless baby that you were! I have gone through much for
you, knowing that I would never have a son of my own.
I made you my son, Achilles, so that in my hour of need
you might save me from destruction. So now, Achilles, I
say, rule your pride, do not be angry forever. Even the
very gods themselves let themselves be won over and they
are greater and have more power than men. For Prayers

are the daughters of Zeus, and with down-turned eyes they walk in the footsteps of Sin. But Sin is strong and swift. He far outruns them and goes all over the face of the earth, making men fall, and then Prayers come after to make things better if they can. And if a man will hear them it will be well with him when he prays in his turn; but if not, if he makes his heart hard to them, then they go their way to Zeus and pray that Sin and Destruction may be with him to the end. So now, Achilles, hear the daughters of Zeus, the Prayers that all right-minded men respect. For see now, Agamemnon is offering you everything and has sent these, the best of the Greeks, to you. Till now no one could say that you were in the wrong. So now, let your anger die down. It will be harder, later, to save the ships when they are burning. Come now, while there are gifts to be had. Later, if you fight without gifts, there will be no such honor, not even if you save the ships then, as you may."

But swift-footed Achilles answered: "Phoenix, old man, my father, what need have I of this honor? I have honor enough from Zeus, and it will be mine while I breathe and my knees are still strong. So let them take that king, Agamemnon, this my answer. But you will sleep here and at daybreak we will take thought about sailing home or staying here."

So saying, he signed to Patroclus to make a bed ready for Phoenix, so that the others might think of going. And Ajax said: "Let us go, Odysseus, for Achilles has worked up his anger. Any man will take a great enough price, whatever the wrong done him. As for you, Achilles, you have made your heart hard because of one girl only, when we are offering you seven, the best there are, and many other gifts as well. Be more welcoming and keep in mind that we are under your roof. We would still be nearest to you of all the Greeks."

And Achilles answered: "Ajax, all this you say seems to be almost after my own mind; but my heart swells with anger to think what Agamemnon did to me before everybody as though I were some outlaw with no rights. Go and tell him that I will not take up my arms again till Hector comes to my own ships with fire. Then, I think, he will be stopped, however much of a fighter he may be."

Then with both hands to their cups they made their drink offerings and Odysseus and Ajax went their way by the line of ships. But Patroclus told the handmaids to put out a bed for Phoenix and there the old man lay and waited for bright Dawn. But Achilles slept in the inner part of the well-built hut and at his side lay a woman he had brought from Lesbos, fair-faced Diomede. And Patroclus lay on the opposite side, and by him lay Iphis whom Achilles had given to him when he took Scyrus, the high city.

When Odysseus and Ajax came to the huts of Agamemnon the Greeks stood up on this side and that and drank to them out of cups of gold. Agamemnon was the first to question them. And Odysseus told them all.

Long the Greeks kept silence after his words in their sorrow. But at last Diomede of the loud war cry said: "Great King of men, Agamemnon, would you had never sent to unmatched Achilles or offered him such gifts, for now his pride will be still greater. But let him be; let him go or stay as he pleases. For the present let us go to our rest when we have taken meat and wine to make us stronger for tomorrow. And when rose-fingered Dawn comes, then, Agamemnon, get the armies to their stations and fight yourself first among them." Then they made their drink offerings and went every man to his hut and there took the gift of sleep.

In BOOK 10, *omitted in this version, Diomede and Odysseus go out that night to the Trojan camp. They meet Dolon, who has been sent out by Hector to spy on the Greek camp, and kill him. Then they go among the sleeping Thracians and take the horses of Rhesus, the Thracian king.*

11

NOW Dawn came up from her bed at Tithonus' side to bring light to immortals and to mortal men. And Zeus sent Discord to the swift ships of the Greeks with a sign in her hands of war. And she took her stand by Odysseus' ship and shouted. And in the hearts of the Greeks she put courage to fight on. War became sweeter to them than going back home in their hollow ships.

And Agamemnon shouted loud telling the Greeks to get ready for battle, and he made himself ready. The Trojans over against them on the slope of the plain came together about great Hector. As among the clouds a deadly star shows, now bright and now covered by the shadowy clouds, so Hector would show at the front or the back giving his orders. He flashed in his bronze like the lightning of father Zeus.

As reapers cut wheat or barley in a rich man's field and the handfuls fall, so Trojans and Greeks fought together and neither would give ground. And Discord was glad to see it; only she of the gods was with them in their fighting. The other gods were in their fair houses on Olympus, blaming Zeus for wanting to give glory to the Trojans. But he did not care about them. He sat by himself, full of joy in his glory, looking down on the city and the Greek ships, the flashing of the bronze, the killers and the killed.

Now all morning long as the sacred day increased, so long the spears and arrows on both sides hit home and men kept falling, but at the hour when a woodman gets his midday meal ready in the mountains—his arms are tired with cutting down tall trees, and desire for sweet food takes hold of him—then the Greeks broke through the Trojan lines.

But the son of Cronos stretched again a line of battle, as he looked down from Ida, and they kept killing one another. Hector was fighting on the left of the battle by the river Scamander, where most heads were falling round great Nestor and warlike Idomeneus. With these Hector was at play and terrible were the things he did. But the Greeks would not have fallen back if Paris had not hit Machaon, the great surgeon, in the right shoulder. And Idomeneus said to Nestor: "Come, get up in your chariot and quickly take

Machaon to the ships. A surgeon is of more value than many fighting men." And Nestor did so.

Then father Zeus from his high seat sent fear into Telemonian Ajax' heart and he gave ground, holding his great shield at his back, turning about and going slowly backward step by step—even as a yellow lion is driven from the cattle by dogs and countrymen that will not let him take the fattest of the herd, and watch the whole night through; he makes his spring but gets nothing by it, and spears from many a strong hand fall thick about him, and flaming branches as well that are too much for him however hungry he is, and at dawn he goes angry away; so against his will Ajax gave ground before the Trojans, fearing very much for the Greek ships.

And as a donkey—on whose sides many a stick has been broken—is more than a match for boys going by a field of corn—he goes in and wastes the deep grain and the boys hit him as hard as they can with sticks but not hard enough; and they only drive him out of the field when he has had as much as he wanted—so the Trojans and their allies attacked great Ajax, hitting him on his shield with spears and crowding about him. But he kept his heart up and rounding upon them would drive them back and then again slowly give ground. So he kept them from getting, any of them, at the ships. Spears were sticking into his great shield, and many, missing his white body, were planted in the earth about him.

Eurypylus saw that Ajax was nearly overcome by this rain and he came and stood by his side, and threw his spear and hit Apisaon in the liver and loosed his knees, but when he sprang to take Apisaon's armor, godlike Paris saw and hit Eurypylus with an arrow in the right thigh. The arrow broke, but the point was in his thigh. He went back into the mass of the Greeks crying out: "Friends, chiefs, princes, turn and stand and save Ajax who is being overpowered. I doubt if he will come out alive. Stand and face the Trojans around great Ajax." So wounded Eurypylus cried, and they came and stood by him with their shields up and spears high; and Ajax joined them and turned and stood.

They fought on like blazing fire. Achilles was standing by his great ship watching the fighting when Nestor drove by. And he cried out to Patroclus, who heard him and came, and for Patroclus this was the beginning of evil. "Before long now," said Achilles, "I think the Greeks will be standing about my knees in prayer. But go first, Patroclus, and see who is the wounded man that Nestor is taking in his chariot out of the fighting. He looks to me like Machaon, but I did not see his eyes. The horses went past so quickly." And Patroclus ran to Nestor's hut.

When Nestor came to his hut with Machaon they got down and undid the old man's horses and stood in the sea wind drying the sweat in their shirts. Then they went inside and took their seats. And fair-haired Hecamede, who was given as a prize to Nestor when Achilles took the city of Tenedos, mixed them a drink. First she put a table before them and on it she put a bronze vessel with an onion to give a taste to the drink and honey and barley meal. There was a great gold cup there with four handles and two gold birds on each handle feeding, and the woman—beautiful as a goddess, she was—put Pramnian wine in the cup and grains of goat's milk cheese and white barley and when it was ready she told them to drink. Then Patroclus came to the door. When the old man saw him he went and took him by the hand and told him to be seated. But Patroclus stood and said: "I have no time, sir. Achilles sent me to see whom you were bringing home wounded and now I must go back and tell him it is Machaon. You know what a hard man he is, and how ready he is to blame even where there is no cause."

And Nestor answered: "Why does Achilles care which of the Greeks are wounded? It is nothing to him that all our best men are in the ships now down with arrow and spear wounds: Diomede and Odysseus and Agamemnon himself and Eurypylus, too, with an arrow in his thigh. Is Achilles going to wait till the ships are on fire, and they kill us one on top of another? I am not as strong as I used to be. In the old days . . . I sprang on them like a black storm and fifty chariots I took and by every chariot two men bit the earth with their teeth under my spear . . . and I killed the very last man of them and all gave praise—to Zeus among gods and to Nestor among men. That is the sort of man I was in those days, if ever there was one. . . . I could go on about those great times for hours on end. But do you, Patroclus, talk to Achilles, as your father told you to. I and Odysseus heard what he told you when Peleus was sending you both to Agamemnon. We two were inside, I and Odysseus, and we heard it all even as he said it. We had come to Peleus' well-built house, getting the army together all through Greece, we were. And we found Menoetius, your father, and you in the house, and Achilles was with you. The old man Peleus was outside in the court before the house, burning the thighs of a bull to Zeus, the thunderbolt thrower, and he had a golden cup in his hand and was pouring wine to go with the burnt offering. You two were working on the bull, and then we came and stood in the doorway. And Achilles, surprised, got up and took us by the hand and told us to be seated and gave us a very good welcome, everything it is right to give to strangers. Old Peleus told Achilles to be always the bravest and best of all fighters, but what Menoetius told you was this. He said: 'My child, Achilles is greater by birth than you are, but you are older, though he is much the stronger. Your part is to talk to him wisely. Make him see what is the right thing to do, and he will profit from it.' Those were your father's orders to you; you have not kept them in mind. But even now why don't you make another attempt? With Heaven's help you might move his heart. He may be keeping back from something he has heard of through his mother. If so, why don't you let him at least send you out with the Myrmidons? And put his armor on. The Trojans might take you for him and back out of the battle. That might give us the breathing space we need. You are untired and they are tired out with fighting. It would not be hard for you to drive them back to their city away from the ships and huts."

With these words in his heart Patroclus ran back by the line of ships to Achilles. On his way he saw Eurypylus coming wounded out of the fighting with the arrowhead in his thigh. Sweat ran down from his head and shoulders and black blood came from the cruel wound, but his mind was clear. He said to Patroclus: "There is no more hope for the Greeks. They will fall among the ships. All the best of them are wounded and the Trojans are getting stronger all the time. But save me. Take me to the ship, cut this arrow out of my leg, wash the blood from it with warm water and put the right things on it—the plants they say you have learned about from Achilles who learned about them from Cheiron, the best of the Centaurs."

And Patroclus answered: "What can we do, Eurypylus? I am taking a word from Nestor to Achilles. Still, even so, I must do the best I can for you." And he put his arm round him and helped him into his hut and a servant put skins on the floor. Then Patroclus took a knife and cut the sharp arrowhead from his leg and washed the black blood away with warm water. Then he crushed a bitter root—rubbing it between his hands—and put it on the wound. The root took away all the pain. The blood stopped and the wound dried.

12

THE GREEKS were herded in at their ships in fear of Hector and he fought on as before like a storm wind. As when a wild boar or lion, in the joy of his strength, rounds upon dogs and men, and these stand round him like a wall and throw their spears at him; but his courage keeps up though his high heart will be the death of him; and he wheels on them and they fall back wherever he attacks: even so fought Hector.

But the horses would not go across the ditch; loudly they neighed standing on its edge. It was too wide to be jumped or to drive across and at the far edge were the sharp-pointed stakes the Greeks had planted, a defense against attackers.

Then Polydamas went to Hector and said: "It would be foolish to attempt to go across with our chariots; we would be in a very bad position, for the Greeks might well turn on us, while we are mixed up in the ditch. I want to crush them as much as anyone, but if we do not take care here, not one of us will get back alive to Troy to tell the story. Let the chariot drivers hold our horses on this side, while you, Hector, show us the way on foot. The Greeks will not be able to stand against us, if it is true that their hour has come."

Polydamas' counsel pleased Hector, and he sprang from his chariot and so did they all. Then they attacked in five companies. The first Hector and Polydamas headed, with Cebriones, Hector's chariot driver, as a third. Hector gave his horses over to a less brave man than Cebriones. The second company was under Paris; the third under Helenus and Deïphobos, sons of Priam. Aeneas headed the fourth and Sarpedon the fifth, made up of the glorious allies. He took with him Glaucus and Asteropaeus, who seemed to him the bravest of all after himself, for he was the best man even in the whole army. These, then, guarding one another with their shields, attacked on foot, certain that the Greeks would hold out no longer.

But as the young men with Polydamas and Hector, the strongest and bravest of the companies, were still at the edge of the ditch, doubts came upon them, for they saw a sign. A great bird, an eagle gripping a blood-red snake, came sailing over them. And the snake was still alive and fighting and biting the eagle's breast, till the eagle, in pain, let it fall there among them; and he himself, with a loud cry, went off down wind. The Trojans shook with fear to see this snake among them, taking it to be an evil sign from Zeus.

Then Polydamas turned to brave Hector and said: "Hector, you will never hear me, even when what I say is wise. You think it is a bad thing for one of the people to take another side from yours and would have him only support you. Nevertheless, I must say now what I think. Let us not go forward to fight with the Greeks for the ships. For this thing was a sign and I see from it what will take place. The eagle let go his hold; he did not take the snake home to his little ones; even so, though we break through the gate and the wall in our strength, we will go back again by the same road and not in good order. Any seer would tell you this is what the sign says."

Then with an angry look Hector said to him: "Polydamas, this is no longer to my pleasure. You can find a better reading of the sign than that. If you are serious you must be out of your senses, telling me to go against the counsels of loud-thundering Zeus, and the words to which he bent his head, but be overruled by a long-winged bird. What do I care which way they fly, toward dawn or dark, on my right hand or on my left? Let us believe in the counsel of great Zeus, king over all mortals and immortals. One omen is best, to fight for our country. Why are you so afraid of war and battle? If the rest of us are to be killed at the ships, you will not, for you are not a man of courage who puts himself in danger. Still, if you hold back, or attempt to turn others back from the fighting, here is my spear ready to take your life."

So saying, he went on, and Zeus, the thunderbolt thrower, sent down from Ida a storm wind that blew the dust thick over the Greek ships. So he blinded the Greeks and gave glory to the Trojans and Hector. And they went to work now to pull down the wall, dragging at its supports, hoping to open a way through it. But the Greeks did not give way and threw everything they had at the Trojans as they came up under the wall.

The two Ajaxes went everywhere on the walls urging on the Greeks, saying honeyed words to some and hard words to others when they saw anyone fall back. "O friends," they cried, "good fighters or bad or in between, for men cannot all be equal in battle, there is work enough here for us all; you know it yourselves. Let there be no turning back to the ships now; keep one another in heart. It may be that Zeus, Lord of the lightning, will help us now to throw them back and drive them toward the city."

So these lifted up the Greeks' spirits. As flakes of snow fall thick on a winter day, when Zeus, the counselor, is moved to snowing, and sends these arrows of his among men; and he quiets the winds and snows on, hour after hour, till he has covered the tops of the mountains and the high headlands and the rich fields of men; and over the harbors and the edges of the gray sea the snow lies deep, but the wave as it rolls keeps it off; all other things are weighted down by the storm of Zeus; even so from both sides stones flew thick from Trojans and from Greeks as they threw at one another.

But the Trojans and glorious Hector would not have broken down the gates if Zeus had not turned his son Sarpedon against the Greeks, like a lion against cattle. With his gold-threaded shield before him, and waving his two spears in the air, he went at the Greeks as a mountain lion, who has had no meat for days, will break into a well-built sheepfold to attack the sheep. He may find the shepherds with their dogs and spears are keeping watch over them, but he is in no mind to be driven away till he has either taken one or himself been hit by a spear from some swift hand; so did his soul urge on Sarpedon. And he said to Glaucus, son of Hippolochus: "Why are we two held in honor, given the first places, and the best meat and full cups in Lycia, while men look up to us as gods? And wide fields are ours, too, by the banks of Xanthus, and fair apple trees and far-stretching plowland. For this we must now take our stand at the head of the Lycians and face the Greeks before them, so that one may say to another: 'Truly these men who rule in Lycia are not inglorious. They eat fat sheep and drink the best of wine; but they are strong, for they fight among the first in battle.' Ah, friend, if when we were through this fight we could live on getting no older forever, I would neither fight myself nor send you into the battle. But death in a thousand shapes hangs over us always. So let us go forward, to win glory or give it to another."

So he said, and the two went forward heading the Lycians. But Teucer the bowman hit Glaucus with an arrow from the high wall where he saw his arm uncovered, and stopped his fighting. Back from the wall he sprang secretly, so that no Greek might see that he was wounded and glory over him. And Sarpedon sorrowed for Glaucus but went on fighting. And he took the top of the wall in his strong hands and pulled, and it gave way and he made a road for many.

Then Ajax and Teucer came at him. Teucer hit him with an arrow on his shield but Zeus kept death from him. And Ajax hit him, too, but the spear point did not go in, though it pushed him back. Then Sarpedon turned to the brave Lycians and cried: "What is wrong with you, Lycians? I cannot break through and open a way to the ships by myself. With me, now, for the more men, the better work."

And they in shame joined with him. But neither the Greeks nor the Lycians had the better. They were like two men with measuring rods in hand, at the landmark stones in a common field, each attempting to get a little more space from the other. And many were wounded or killed, and the wall was wet with the blood of men from both sides. As a good hard-working woman, a spinner of wool, puts the weight and the wool in the balance, making them equal, to get what little she can for her children, so equal was their battle, till Zeus gave glory to Hector who was the first to spring inside the wall of the Greeks.

He took up a stone that was lying before the gate, thick at the base but sharp-pointed. Two men, as mortal men are now, would have found it hard to lift it up from the earth into a cart. But for Hector the son of crooked-counseling Cronos made it light. As when a shepherd takes up all a sheep's wool in one hand, and little is the weight of it to him, so Hector lifted up the stone and planted himself well, so that the blow might have full force. The stone broke right through, falling inside, and the doors flew open. Then glorious Hector sprang inside, his face like sudden night; the terrible bronze flashed on his body and in his hands were two spears. No one but a god could have kept him out and his eyes flamed with fire. Turning he cried to the Trojans to come over the wall. Some did and some came through the gate and the Greeks were driven among their ships and loud was the shouting.

In BOOK 13, *not included in this translation, Poseidon comes to the help of the Greeks and the Cretan chief, Idomeneus, has his day of glory, but the Trojans keep on fighting.*

14

THE CRY of battle was not unnoted by Nestor, though he was sitting at his wine, and he said to Machaon: "What now, do you think, Machaon? Those young men are making more noise. But sit where you are over your wine, till fair Hecamede gets a hot bath ready for you to wash off the blood. I will go and see what it is all about."

He took up his son's shield which was lying there in the hut. His son had Nestor's own shield. And with his bronze-pointed spear in his hand he went out. There he saw a sad sight: the Greeks flying before the Trojans and the wall broken down. And, as when the great sea swells darkly without sound, waiting troubled for the sudden winds, but moves uncertainly, rolling in no one direction till the storm comes down from Zeus, so the old man turned this way and that in his mind. In the end, it seemed best to him to go to find Agamemnon.

He met the wounded kings Agamemnon and Diomede and Odysseus as they were coming up from the ships. They were walking together, resting themselves on their spears, and looking on at the battle with sorrow in their hearts. When they met old Nestor things seemed to them even worse. And Agamemnon said: "O Nestor, I fear that Hector will make his word good and not go back to Troy before he has burned our ships and killed us all. That is what he said and now it is all coming true. I think that others of the Greeks must be storing up anger against me like Achilles, with no mind to fight by the ships. It must be Zeus' good pleasure. I knew well when he was helping us, and now he is with the Trojans, giving them godlike glory. But come, let us do as I say. Let us drag down the first line of ships nearest the sea and get them out on the water, anchor them with stones till immortal night comes. But who knows if even then the Trojans will stop fighting. Later we might drag down all the ships. There is nothing wrong in flying from destruction even by night. It is better to fly and be saved than to be taken."

With an angry look Odysseus answered: "What is this from your mouth, Agamemnon? Be silent; do not let any others of the Greeks hear such words, which no man with any sense of right could ever have let fall from his lips, still less a king ruling over so many. I have no longer any respect at all for your judgment. You tell us to drag our ships down to the sea while the battle is still raging, to do, that is, what the Trojans most want and make our complete destruction certain. The Greeks will not go on fighting if we move the ships but will be looking over their shoulders at them all the time and getting out of the battle. Your counsel would be the end of us, O general."

And Agamemnon answered: "Odysseus, your bitter words have pierced my heart. However, I am not for ordering this against the will of the Greeks. But has anyone, young or old, better counsel to offer? It would be welcome."

Then Diomede said: "He is near enough. You need not go looking far off for that, if you are ready to hear me out without getting angry, any one of you, because in years I am the youngest here. You cannot say I am a coward by blood, or a poor fighter, and so pay no attention to my counsel. Let us go down to the battle, wounded though we are. We will keep out of it, not to get wound on wound, but we can urge and send others in to fight, even those who have been nursing their anger and taking no part."

They did as he said, Agamemnon the King walking in front.

Poseidon, the Shaker of Earth, had been keeping no blind watch where he sat wondering at the war, high on the topmost point of wooded Samothrace. From there all Ida was clear to see, and Troy and the Greek ships. He had come from under the sea and taken his seat there, for he pitied the

Greeks, who were being overcome by the Trojans, and he was greatly angered against Zeus.

Now Poseidon came up to them in the form of an old man and took Agamemnon's right hand and said: "Agamemnon, now truly, I think, is Achilles' heart in his breast happy, to see the Greeks being killed. There is no knowledge in him, not a grain. May a god bring him low and he die. But as for you, the gods are not so angered against you that you may not still see the Trojans flying from the ships and huts toward their city." At that he shouted as loud as nine or ten thousand fighters can cry in battle and put in the heart of every Greek great strength to fight on.

Now Hera, standing on Olympus, saw and knew him as her brother and her lord's as well; and her heart was glad. And she saw Zeus seated on the topmost point of Ida, and he was hateful to her heart. She thought hard, did ox-eyed queenly Hera, how she could have her own way and trick him. And this seemed to her best, to go to Ida, after making the most of her person, and see if Zeus would desire to lie by her side in love and if she could make a sweet and gentle sleep come down on his eyelids and his designing mind. So she went to her room, that her dear son Hephaestus had built her with strong doors and a secret lock that no other god could open. She went in and shut the bright doors. Then with ambrosia she washed her fair body and put on it oil, ambrosial, soft, sweet-smelling; and she combed her hair, fair and ambrosial, hanging from her immortal head. Then she put on an ambrosial dress, which Athene had made for her with much beautiful work on it, and pinned it across her breast with gold pins, and put a belt round her and, in her pierced ears, earrings with three berrylike drops. And over her she put a white veil, bright as the sun, and under her feet fair sandals. Then she went from her room and to Aphrodite—away from the other gods—she said: "Will you do what I ask you, dear child? Or are you too angry with me over the way I am helping the Greeks?"

Aphrodite answered: "Queenly goddess, daughter of great Cronos, tell me what it is and I will do it if I can."

Then with designing mind, queenly Hera said: "Give me now love and desire with which you overcome all immortals and mortals. For I am on my way to the limits of the earth, to see Oceanus from whom the gods are sprung, and mother Tethys. How lovingly they nursed and looked after me when they took me away from Rhea, at the time when Zeus thrust Cronos down under the earth and the unresting sea! I am going to them to make peace between them. They are so angry with one another they have not come together in love for a long time. If I can join their hearts in love again, they will be grateful to me forever."

Laughter-loving Aphrodite answered: "I cannot and must not say no, for you sleep in the arms of Zeus, chief of the gods."

And she loosed from her breast that strangely ornamented band in which love and desire and the tricks that take away the senses of the wisest are worked. She gave it to Hera and said: "Take this and you will not come back with anything undone that your heart desires."

And queenly Hera, smiling, put the strangely worked band in her breast.

Aphrodite went to her house, but Hera flew down from Olympus and over Piera and fair Emathia, and over the snowy mountains of the Thracian horsemen, over their highest points, not touching the earth with her feet, and from Athos she went across the sea and came to Lemnos. There she met Sleep, the brother of Death, and she took him by the hand and said: "You who rule over all gods and men, if ever you did what I asked you before, do so again and I will be grateful to you forever. Shut the bright eyes of Zeus for me in sleep while I have him in my arms, and I will give you a beautiful gold seat made for you by Hephaestus, my son, and he will make, too, a footstool to rest your feet on while you drink your wine."

But Sleep answered: "Hera, queenly goddess, any other one of the gods I would very readily put to sleep, even the waters of Oceanus himself from whom they are all sprung; but not Zeus, or only at his own request. Once before a request of yours taught me a lesson, that day when Heracles sailed away after wasting the city of Troy. I put Zeus to sleep for you then, while you worked up the cruel winds against Heracles and drove him over the face of the deep to Cos, far away from all his friends. And Zeus when he was awake again was angry and threw the gods about his house. He was looking for me, most of all, and if Night, who overcomes gods and men, had not saved me, he would have thrown me right out of Heaven into the deep and I would never have been heard of again. Zeus was afraid to anger Night so he gave up looking for me. You are asking more than I can do."

Hera said: "Why do you trouble yourself about such things. Do you think Zeus cares about helping the Trojans as he cared about his own son? Come, I will give you one of the younger Graces for your wife, Pasithea with whom you have been in love so long."

Sleep was glad at this and answered: "Swear to me by the dread waters of Styx, with one hand on the fruitful earth and the other on the bright sea, that all may be witnesses, even the gods who are under all with Cronos, to give me for my wife Pasithea, with whom I have been in love so long."

And Hera did so and swore as he told her to, naming the gods who are under Tartarus, the Titans. Then the two went swiftly from Lemnos and Imbros and, clothed in mist, came to Ida and the tops of the trees waved under their feet as they went. Before Zeus saw him, Sleep stopped at a tall fir tree, the highest on Ida. There among the thick branches he sat in the form of a sweet-singing mountain bird, named by the gods Chalcis, and by men Cymindis.

But Hera went on to topmost Gargarus, the highest point of Ida. And when Zeus saw her, love took hold of his heart as when first they came together without the knowledge of their father and mother. "Hera," he said, "what desire has brought you here from Olympus? And you have no horses or chariot with you!"

With her design in mind, Hera said: "I am going to Oceanus and Tethys, to make peace between them. They are so angry with one another they have not come together in love for a long time. And my horses and chariot stand at the foot of many-springed Ida. I came to see you first, because you might be angry with me if I went so far away without saying a word."

Then Zeus, the cloud-bringer, answered: "You can go there later, Hera. But now, the two of us, let us take our joy together in love. Never did desire for any goddess or mortal woman so overcome the heart in my breast. No, not even for Ixion's wife, or Danae, or Phoenix' daughter, or Semele, or Alcmene the mother of Heracles, or fair-haired Demeter, or glorious Leto, or even your own self. So much now I love you and sweet desire takes hold of me."

And Hera answered: "Most dread son of Cronos, what is this you are saying? Here in the open on the top of Ida. What if one of the gods saw us and told all the other gods? I could never face them again. But if this is your pleasure, you have a room which your own son Hephaestus built with strong doors on the doorposts. Let us go there if that is your desire."

Zeus answered: "Do not be afraid that any god or man will see us. I will make such a thick golden cloud that the Sun himself cannot see us."

With that he took his wife in his arms and under them the earth sent up young grass, thick and soft, with every sort of sweet flowers, which held them up as they lay. And they were covered by a fair golden cloud from which bright dewdrops fell.

So in quiet on topmost Gargarus, the father, by sleep and

love overcome, held his wife in his arms. But sweet Sleep
ran to the Greek ships to give news of this to Poseidon, and
Poseidon cried to the Greeks: "Are you ready to give in
to Hector, to let him take the ships and win himself glory,
because Achilles is still nursing his anger? But we will do
very well without him if we help one another. Come now
after me. Hector will not stand against us." And he him-
self went first with a long-edged sword in his hand, like the
lightning it was, that no man may use in battle. Then truly
the cords of war were stretched to the full. Not so loud is
the great wave of the sea when it is driven in by the North
Wind, or a forest fire on the mountains, or the wind in the
high crests of the oaks, at the loudest of its rage, as the shout-
ing then of the Greeks and Trojans, springing one upon an-
other.

Hector, first, threw his spear at Ajax and did not miss him
but hit him where his sword belt and shield band went across
his breast and they kept the spear out. But as Hector sprang
back among the Trojans, great Telemonian Ajax hit him
with a stone. There were many great stones, supports to
the ships, about, lying under their feet as they fought. One
of these he lifted and hit Hector with it over the edge of
his shield on the neck and sent him whirling round and
round. As an oak falls uprooted under the thunderbolt of
Zeus—and no one has the courage to look on, so dread is the
bolt—so in the dust great Hector fell. His spear fell from
his hand, and his shield and helmet and bronze armor rang
from the fall. With loud shouts the Greeks ran up, hoping
to drag him off, and throwing their spears, but no one could

wound him before the bravest of the Trojans ran forward to keep them off, Polydamas and Aeneas and Agenor and Sarpedon, chief of the Lycians and unmatched Glaucus with him. The others, too, were not slow to help but held up their round shields to cover him. Then they lifted him in their arms and took him out of the battle to where his swift horses were waiting. And when they came to the fair river, eddying Xanthus, they lifted him down from the chariot and poured water over him. And he breathed and looked up and kneeling on his knees brought up black blood. Then he fell back again on the earth, and night covered his eyes; his spirit was still overcome by the blow.

But when the Greeks saw Hector going out of the fighting they raged the more and each man of the Trojans looked about him for a way to escape destruction, for Poseidon had turned the battle.

15

THE TROJANS were across the wall and ditch, and many were dead in their flight, before they stopped, white with fear, where the horses and chariots were lined up. Then Zeus awoke on Ida by Hera's side. And he sprang up and saw the Trojans in flight and Poseidon among the Greeks, driving them on and Hector breathing in pain, and bringing up blood, for it was not the least of the Greeks who had hit him. Seeing him, the father of gods and men had pity, and with a dread look he said to Hera: "All this is your evil doing. I do not know that the first fruits will not be yours from my whip. Bring to mind when I hung you up with two anvils fixed to your feet, and not one of the gods could free you however angry about it they were. I threw them from Heaven to earth if they came near. That was for what you did to Heracles and the way you tricked me then."

And Hera shook with fear and said: "Earth be my witness and wide Heaven and the waters of Styx, the greatest and most dread oath for the gods, and your own sacred head, and our marriage bed, by which I would never swear falsely: it is not by my will that Poseidon is punishing the Trojans and Hector, and helping the Greeks. It is his own soul and his pity for them which urge him on. I would counsel even him to do as you, Lord of the storm cloud, tell him."

And Zeus smiled and said: "If what you say is true, go find me Iris. Let her go and tell Poseidon from me to stop fighting and get home; and let Phoebus Apollo put strength into Hector again and drive back the Greeks in flight till they fall among the ships of Achilles. Then Achilles will send out Patroclus. Hector will kill him with the spear before Troy after Patroclus has killed many other young men, and among them my own son, Sarpedon. Then in anger for Patroclus Achilles will kill Hector. And after that the Greeks will take Troy by the counsels of Athene. But let no immortal now help the Greeks. First must my word be done which I gave to Thetis and I bent my head to it, to do honor to Achilles, waster of cities."

Driven back again among their ships, the Greeks lifted their hands in prayer, but most of all Nestor, stretching out his two hands to the starry Heaven. "O father Zeus, if ever any man of us in Argos burned to you fat thighs of bull

or ram, praying that he might come home again, and you
bent your head, now keep death from us and do not let the
ships be overrun by the Trojans."

So he prayed, and Zeus, the counselor, heard the old man's
prayer and thundered.

The Trojans, when they heard the thunder, sprang still
more fiercely on the Greeks. As a great wave of the wide-
wayed sea comes down over the side of a ship when the sea
runs high before the wind, whose force lifts up the waves,
so with a great cry down came the Trojans over the wall to
the ships; and the Greeks, high up on the decks of their
black ships, fought them off with the long pikes they had
on the ships for sea fighting.

Now Patroclus was sitting with kindly Eurypylus, talk-
ing to him and putting things on his wound to take away the
pain. But when he saw the Trojans come over the wall, he
hit his two thighs with the flat of his hands and moaned and
said: "Eurypylus, you need me badly, I know; but I must
go. A servant can take care of you now. I must run quickly
to Achilles and get him to fight. With Heaven's help I
may be able to move him."

Now Ajax was springing over the decks of the Greek
ship, in his hands a long sea fighter's pike jointed with rings
thirty feet or more long. As a truly good horseman may
drive four horses together from a plain on a highway to-
ward a great city, and many wonder at him, men and
women; with light step he springs from horse to horse as
they run on; so Ajax kept springing from one deck to an-
other of the many ships and his voice went up to Heaven.

With terrible cries he shouted to the Greeks to fight for their ships and huts. And Hector, as an eagle drops on water birds feeding by a river's bank, made straight for a black ship; it brought Protesilaus to Troy but did not take him home; and held onto it crying: "Bring fire! Now has Zeus given us the day that makes up for all."

And they fought the harder, so that Ajax gave way a little, but he watched and with his long spear he guarded the ship. And whoever would run upon the ship with flaming fire, as Hector ordered, he would wait for and wound him with a thrust; twelve men he wounded so in the fight at the ships.

16

🔲🔲🔲🔲🔲🔲🔲🔲🔲🔲🔲🔲🔲🔲🔲🔲🔲🔲🔲🔲🔲🔲🔲🔲🔲🔲🔲🔲🔲🔲🔲🔲🔲🔲🔲🔲🔲🔲

THEY were fighting round Protesilaus' ship by the time Patroclus got back to Achilles. And he came up to him in tears. As dark water runs down over the face of a cliff, so were his tears. And Achilles saw his tears and said: "Why, Patroclus, what is this? Why are you all tears like a little girl, a baby, running by her mother's side, pulling at her dress and praying to be lifted up? What is it? Is it bad news? Your father or mine—are they dead? We would feel sorrow, and deeply, if they were. Or can you be sorrowing for the Greeks who are being killed now at the ships through their own injustice?"

Then Patroclus answered. "O Achilles, strongest of the

Greeks, do not be angry. So many of the best of them are
down wounded by spear or arrow—Diomede and Odys-
seus and Agamemnon among them, and Eurypylus with an
arrow in his thigh—and we are doing what we can for their
wounds. But what about you, Achilles? Never may such
anger as this grow in me, O you only good for the wound-
ing of others. Your father, it seems, was not Peleus nor
Thetis your mother, but the gray sea and the black cliffs
gave you birth, so cruel and hard is your heart. If it is some
word from Zeus that holds you back, send me out with the
Myrmidons. Let me put on your armor and go out in your
place. The Trojans maybe will take me for you and back
out of the battle. That might give us the breathing space
we need. It won't be hard for untired men like us to drive
the tired-out Trojans back to their city and save the ships
and huts."

So he said, unknowing that it was his own death and fate
he was praying for. Then, his heart deeply moved, swift-
footed Achilles answered: "Ah, Patroclus. What is this you
have said! No word from Zeus holds me back. Only I am
cut to the heart that a man like Agamemnon could take my
prize from me, as if I were an outlaw who has no rights.
But let these things be, as past and done. I did not think I
would make an end of my anger before the war cry and the
battle came to my own ships. Put on my armor and take out
the war-loving Myrmidons to the fight and fall upon the
Trojans and drive them from the ships. The dark cloud
of the Trojans is all about us and these other Greeks have
nothing but the sea now to support them and little enough

space of land. The whole city of Troy has come down with-
out fear against them, for they do not see the front of my
helmet before them. They would quickly fill up the river
beds with their dead in their flight, if King Agamemnon had
been kindly toward me. But now they are warring all
round us. Diomede is no longer fighting and so far I have
not heard Agamemnon's voice shouting from his hated head.
No, it is the voice of man-killing Hector that rings in my
ears as he gives his orders, and they overthrow the Greeks
in battle. But take this to heart. Come back again when you
have cleared the ships. Do not go up against Troy or you
will make my honor less. And one of the gods that are for-
ever may come down from Olympus against you—for
dearly does Phoebus Apollo love them. So come back when
you have saved the ships and let the rest fight across the
plain. For, O father Zeus and Athene and Apollo, O would
that not one of the Trojans, not one of them all—nor one of
the Greeks—might escape death, if only we two together
might throw down the sacred walls of Troy."

As they talked, Ajax could no longer keep his place on
the ship for the throwing spears which came, like rain, upon
him. The will of Zeus and the spears of the Trojans were
too much for him. On his helmet and on the plates over his
face came blow upon blow from them. His left arm grew
tired with keeping up his shield so long. But he would not
go back. His breath came hard, the sweat rained off every
inch of his body, there was no rest for a second; from all
sides danger after danger came at him. And then Hector
came near and with his sword he cut off the point of Ajax'

long pike, and Ajax had in his hand nothing better than a stick. Far off the head of bronze fell ringing on the earth.

And Ajax knew, in his great heart, what Zeus who thunders on high was doing. So he went back under the rain of spears. And then the Trojans threw on the swift ship fire that is never tired.

At that, Achilles hit his thighs with his hands and cried: "Up, Patroclus, up before they take the ships. Put on my armor quickly and I will get my Myrmidons together." Then Patroclus put on Achilles' armor and made himself ready. Only the spear that Cheiron, the Centaur, cut in the mountains for Peleus, Achilles' father, he did not take, for this no other of the Greeks than Achilles could use, so heavy and great and strong it was, the Pelean spear. But Patroclus told Automedon to put the horses to quickly. And Automedon, that Patroclus honored most after Achilles, brought the horses: Xanthus and Balius, swift as the winds, horses born by the Harpy Podarge to the West Wind in the fields by the river Oceanus. And with them he put the horse, Pedasus, that Achilles took when he wasted the city of Eëtion, and he, though mortal, kept up with the immortal horses.

But Achilles went about through the huts urging on the Myrmidons and giving them their orders. And he went into his hut and opened a fair chest which Thetis had put on his ship, full of wool clothing to keep out the wind. There he kept a cup which he used for drink offerings poured to Zeus only of all the gods. He took the cup from the chest and made it clean first with sulphur, then washed it with water, and himself washed his hands and put in it dark wine. Then he prayed, standing in the middle of the space before his ship; and Zeus, who throws the thunder-bolt, had his eye on him. "King Zeus, as once before you heard my voice in prayer, and honored me, sending great sorrows on the Greeks, now again give me this, my desire. Patroclus I send, with my Myrmidons, to war. Let him have his will with the Trojans. But when he has driven them from the ships let him come back here unwounded and with all his arms, he and his friends, my hand-to-hand fighters." So he prayed and Zeus heard his prayer. Part of it he answered, but not all. He let Patroclus drive the Trojans from the ships; he did not let him come back safely out of the fighting.

Then Patroclus and the Myrmidons sprang in high hope upon the Trojans. Out they poured like wasps of the road-side that foolish boys make angry, troubling them in their nests, and if some man on his journey goes by, out the wasps fly one and all with courage high and fight in defense of their young; so the Myrmidons poured out from their ships and great was the shouting. And Patroclus cried: "On for the honor of Achilles! Now let wide-ruling Agamemnon see how blind he was when he honored not at all the best of the Greeks." And when the Trojans saw him, in the bright armor of Achilles, the hearts of all of them were moved, for they thought that Achilles had put by his anger and each man looked about him to see how he might escape destruc-tion. Then Patroclus drove them from the ships and put out the burning fire. As when from the crest of a high mountain, Zeus, thrower of the lightning, has driven a great cloud away and all the cliffs and hollows stand clear and from Heaven breaks open the limitless air, so the Greeks took breath for a little, but still the fighting went on.

Then death came to many on both sides in hateful war. As when from Olympus a cloud comes across Heaven out of the bright air, and Zeus stretches out the storm, so from the ships again the Trojans ran back shouting, and in bad order they went across the ditch again. And Hector knew that the day was now going against him, though he still stood firm helping the others. Then straight over the ditch jumped the swift immortal horses and it was against Hector that Patroclus urged them. But his own swift horses took Hector away. As under a storm the whole black earth is bent, on a day when Zeus is pouring down the rain most violently, angry with men who give crooked judgments in the meeting place and drive justice out, with no thought that the gods can punish; and all the rivers overrun their banks and down the mountainsides the waters cut in deeply and cover the plain with foam on their way to the dark sea, wasting the fields of men; even so was the flight of the Trojan chariots.

But when Sarpedon saw his Lycians being overthrown at the hands of Patroclus, he cried: "Shame on you Lycians! Are you so swift now? I myself will meet this man and know who he is who has loosed the knees of so many."

He sprang from his chariot and Patroclus, seeing him, sprang down, too. And like two great eagles that fight with loud cries on some high cliff, so they flew at one another. And the son of crooked-counseling Cronos had pity when he saw them and said to Hera, his sister and wife: "Now, alas, it is his fate for Sarpedon, dearest of men to me, to be killed by Patroclus. And I have two thoughts in counsel to take him up still living and put him down in the rich land of Lycia far from this sorrowful war; or to kill him now at Patroclus' hands."

To which Hera said: "Dread son of Cronos, what is this you have said? Would you save from death a mortal man, whose hour has long been fixed by fate? Do as you will, but know that we other gods are not with you in this. And take this to heart, too. If you send Sarpedon living to his house, some other god will certainly be minded to send his own dear son safe out of the battle. There are many sons of immortals warring around Troy. So there will be great anger among the gods. If he is so dear to you, let him be killed, but afterward let Death and sweet Sleep take him to wide Lycia, and there let his brothers and friends give him mound and pillar as is the right of the dead."

And the father of gods and men did as she said. But he sent raindrops of blood on the earth in honor of Sarpedon, who was now to be killed in the deep-soiled land of Troy, far from his own country.

Then Patroclus threw and hit Sarpedon's driver Thrasymelus and loosed his knees. But Sarpedon in his turn missed, hitting the horse Pedasus on the right shoulder, and down the horse fell in the dust with a moan, and his life went from him. The other two pulled this way and that till Automedon got down and cut the dead horse loose. Then the two fighters came together again.

Sarpedon missed again, his bright spear going over Patroclus' left shoulder. But Patroclus hit with his bronze near to Sarpedon's heart. He fell as an oak falls, or poplar or tall fir, that men cut down with sharp axes on the mountainside to be used by the shipbuilder; even so he lay outstretched before his horses, moaning and gripping the blood-marked dust. And he cried to his Lycian friend: "Dear Glaucus, now bring up the Lycians to fight for my body. A shame and a hanging of the head all your days I will be to you if the Greeks take my armor." Death came as he said it.

Dread sorrow overcame Glaucus to hear him, for he could not help. The wound in his arm from Teucer's arrow kept him out of the fighting. Holding it in his hand now, he prayed to Apollo. "Hear me, O King, wherever you are, in Lycia or Troy, who can everywhere hear those in sorrow, as I now am in sorrow. My arm is pierced through with sharp pains and the blood still comes from the wound. I cannot hold my spear or fight, so heavy my shoulder is. But do you, O King, make my wound well, and make my pains sleep so that with my Lycians I may fight on over Sarpedon's body."

Phoebus Apollo heard him and made him well and Glaucus knew and was glad. He first got the Lycians together and then went to the Trojans and they fought long with the Greeks over Sarpedon. And like the noise of woodcutters in the hollows of the mountains, and the sound may be heard from far away, so was the noise on their shields as they thrust at one another with swords and two-edged spears. Even a friend could not have known Sarpedon, so covered over he was with spears and blood and dust from head to foot. They came together over him as on a farm the flies buzz around the white milk in spring. But Zeus looked down on all this without ever turning his eyes away. And he had two thoughts in his mind about the death of Patroclus: to let glorious Hector kill him then and there, or to let Patroclus first drive on toward Troy and take the lives of many. And this seemed to him best, to put fear in Hector's heart, and Hector turned in flight. And the Lycians went with him. So Patroclus took Sarpedon's armor from his shoulders and sent it back to the hollow ships. But then Zeus said to Apollo: "Go make Sarpedon clean from the dark blood, and wash him in the river and put ambrosia on him and ambrosial clothing and give him to the swift brothers, Sleep and Death, to take him quickly to the rich lands of wide Lycia. There his brothers and his friends will give him mound and pillar, as is the right of the dead." And Apollo did this.

But Patroclus, blinded in heart, raged on after the Trojans and Lycians. If he had kept Achilles' order in mind he would have escaped black death. But the purpose of Zeus is always stronger than that of men, and he it was who now put rage in Patroclus' breast. And he would have taken high-gated Troy itself, but Apollo stood on the well-built wall and helped the Trojans. Three times Patroclus fought his way up the wall and each time Apollo forced his bright shield back with immortal hands. But when Patroclus was coming up like a god a fourth time, Apollo shouted terribly: "Turn back, Patroclus; it is not for you to take Troy, nor even for Achilles—a better man by far than you." At that Patroclus gave ground.

Then Apollo went and stood by Hector in the form of Asios, Hector's uncle, and said: "Why are you not fighting, Hector? It is not like you! If I were as much stronger than you as I am weaker, you would be feeling my spear by now. Turn your horses against Patroclus and see if you can kill him and get honor from Apollo." Saying this, Apollo sent fear among the Greeks.

Against Patroclus, Hector turned his strong-footed horses. Patroclus sprang from his chariot with his spear in his left hand and in his right he took up a sharp-edged stone. He threw it with all his force and hit Cebriones, Hector's chariot driver, between the eyes, and broke the bone in, and his eyes fell in the dust at his feet and he dropped dead from his chariot like a diver. Over him loudly you cried, horseman Patroclus: "See, see, how well he dives! If we were at sea, how well he would fish up oysters for us—all we could eat—so beautifully he dived out of his chariot here. What divers these Trojans are!" So crying, he sprang on the dead Cebriones like a lion, while Hector sprang from his chariot on the other side. They fought over Cebriones like two lions fighting over a deer killed in the mountains, both hungry, both highhearted. And with them the Greeks and Trojans fought, like the East and South Winds fighting in a mountain wood, shaking the trees till you hear the branches being broken. Many throwing spears fell about Cebriones, and many arrows were loosed from the string and many great stones hit the shields of the fighters; but there in the clouds of dust between them he lay, caring no longer about his driving.

While the sun was high the fighting went on and men were killed, but when the time of the unloosing of oxen came, the Greeks grew much the stronger. They pulled Cebriones out of the hands of the Trojans and took the armor off his body. Then Patroclus sprang like Ares upon the Trojans, crying a terrible cry. Three times he killed nine men, and was coming on again a fourth time, like a god. But then, Patroclus, came the end of life for you. For Apollo met you in the battle. He was covered in thick mist, and Patroclus did not see him. He hit Patroclus on the back with the flat of his hand, so that Patroclus' eyes were blinded and his helmet rolled under the feet of the horses and the horsehair crest was dirtied with blood. And his strong spear was broken in his hands and his shield fell to the ground and Apollo, the prince, the son of Zeus, undid his armor. Then a Trojan, young Euphorbus, put a sharp throwing spear into his back. And then Hector came at him from between the Trojans and drove his spear right through him. He fell and great sorrow came upon the Greeks.

Then Hector cried: "Patroclus! You were going to waste Troy, were you! And take our women away as slaves in your ships. Ah, no, Patroclus, I was between them and you, and now it is the birds who will get you! Little good to you was Achilles who, I think, gave you this order: 'Do not come back to the hollow ships till you have pierced man-killing Hector to the heart, and made his shirt red with his blood.'" And Patroclus answered: "To you, Hector, Zeus and Apollo gave me over, for they took my armor from me themselves. But if twenty like you had faced me, my spear would have killed them all. No, it was Fate and Apollo, and of men Euphorbus, who killed me. You came third. Truly, you yourself will not live long. Death stands near you at the hands of Achilles."

Saying this, his eyes were shut in death and his soul went down to Hades in sorrow.

In BOOK 17, *omitted in this version, Trojans and Greeks fight on all day over Patroclus' body: "as men stretch the skin of a great bull standing round it in a circle and pulling at it from all sides, so they pulled at the dead man." Many are killed but in the end the Greeks are still attempting to bring the body out of the battle.*

18

⌐⌐

OVER Patroclus' body the Greeks and Trojans were fighting like flaming fire, when Antilochus, the good runner, Nestor's son, brought the news of his death to Achilles.

He found him waiting before his horned ships and now fearing the worst. Antilochus came up and his hot tears were falling as he said: "The news is bitter that you must hear, Achilles. Patroclus is killed and they are fighting over his body, for Hector has his armor."

A black cloud of sorrow came upon Achilles as he heard. With both hands he took up dark dust and poured it over his head and face. And he threw himself down in the dust, pulling at his hair with his hands. The women that he and Patroclus had taken ran, crying aloud, around him, and Antilochus in tears took Achilles' hands in his for fear he would cut his throat with his knife. And Achilles moaned in his sorrow, so that his mother Thetis heard him, as she sat deep under the sea by the side of her old father. She cried out and all the goddess-daughters of Nereus that were in the deep of the sea came about her. She cried to them: "Alas, sister nereids, my son, matchless and brave, first of fighters; I brought him up like a young tree in a rich orchard. Never again may I welcome him back to his home, the house of Peleus; and now while he still lives in the light of the sun, he sorrows; and though I go to him, I cannot help him." And she went up through the waves and stepped upon the sand where the ships of the Myrmidons were pulled up in lines. And she took his head in her hands and cried: "My son! What sorrow has come upon your heart? Has not Zeus done as you prayed? Did you not stretch your hands out to pray that all the Greeks might be driven in upon their very ships and undergo cruel things?"

Then swift-footed Achilles answered: "My mother, Zeus has done as I prayed, but what pleasure is that to me? Patroclus is dead whom I honored as no other, even as my own self. And Hector, who killed him, has taken his armor —armor that the gods gave to Peleus on the day you were married to him. O that you had stayed where you were among the immortal daughters of the sea and that Peleus had taken some mortal woman for his bride. But now meas-ureless sorrow will be yours for your dead son. You will never welcome him again to his home. My own heart will not let me live on among men. But Hector first, killed by my spear, must pay for Patroclus' death."

Then Thetis in tears said to him: "You will be short-lived then, my son; for, after Hector's death, yours will come quickly."

Then, greatly moved, Achilles answered: "Let it come, for I was not there to help Patroclus. Far from his own land he was killed and I was not with him in his need. Now because I, too, will never see my own country again, and because I was not there to save Patroclus—or any of my brothers-in-arms that Hector has killed—but was here by the ships, a useless weight on the earth: I that in war am such as no other of the Greeks—now would that war itself might end among gods and men, and anger that sweeter far than drops of honey swells like smoke in men's breasts. Even so did Agamemnon anger me. But now I will go to look for Hector who killed the man I loved, and as for my fate, let it come when Zeus wills and the other immortal gods. I will make many of the deep-breasted Trojan women wipe the tears from their faces with both hands, endlessly moaning, and know well that I have come back into the war. Do not hope to hold me back from the battle, if you love me; for you will not move me."

Then answered the goddess, silver-footed Thetis: "It is well to save your friends from destruction. But your bright armor is Hector's now. Wait then till I come again. In the morning I will have new armor for you, made by Hephaestus."

So saying she turned from him and said to her sisters of the sea: "Dive now down into the deep and go tell all to the old man of the sea, our father, while I go to the house of Hephaestus on high Olympus to see if he will give me glorious armor for my son."

But the Greeks could not take Patroclus' body away, for again the Trojan chariots overtook them, and Hector, in Achilles' armor, was fighting like a flame. Three times he came up and took hold of Patroclus' feet, and three times the two Ajaxes threw him back. But he came again, and would have dragged it away and won great glory, if swift Iris had not come to Achilles from Hera, unknown to Zeus and the other gods. She said: "Achilles, lift up your soul and take help to Patroclus. Men are killing one another in defense of his body. The Trojans would drag it away and Hector most of all; his heart tells him to cut off the head and fix it on a stake on Troy wall; up, then; lie here no more! The shame would be yours if Patroclus became the sport of the dogs of Troy."

Achilles answered: "Goddess Iris, who of the gods sent you to me?"

Iris said: "Hera sent me. Zeus and the others do not know of my coming."

And Achilles answered: "But how can I go into the battle. My mother told me to wait till she came again bringing new armor from Hephaestus. I could use no other armor, except maybe Telemonian Ajax' shield. But he, I think, is in the battle now using it in defense of dead Patroclus."

And she said: "We know well that they have your armor.

But even as you are, come to the ditch and show yourself
to the Trojans. It may be they will be afraid and the Greeks
get time to take breath. There is little breathing space in
war."

And Achilles went, and round his great shoulders Athene
put her dread aegis, and a golden cloud over his head. As
when a smoke is seen from far off going up to Heaven from
an island city that is being attacked, and the townsmen fight
all day long from the city walls, and at the going down of
the sun out come the watch fires one after another, flaming
high for those who live near to see and to bring help if they
can, even so flamed a light from Achilles' head as he stood
by the ditch outside the wall; but he did not join the fight-
ing, keeping his mother's order in mind. He stood there and
shouted, and Athene added her voice, and, hearing, the
hearts of all were afraid. Three times he shouted and three
times the Trojans and allies were shaken. But the Greeks
with glad hearts brought Patroclus out from among the
spears and Achilles went with them to the ships in tears.
Then Hera sent the untiring Sun, unwilling though he was,
to go his way to the waters of Oceanus. So the Greeks rested
from the evil war.

The Trojans undid their horses and came together for
a council before getting their supper ready. They kept
on their feet, with no heart to sit down; they had seen
Achilles and were afraid, though he had kept out of the
fighting so long. Then wise Polydamas, the one among them
who looked before and after, had the first word. He was
Hector's brother-in-arms, born in the same night with

him, one was the best in counsel and the other with the spear. He said: "Think both sides of this over, my friends. I urge you to go back now to the city and not wait here near the ships for morning, far away from our walls. While this man kept out of the battle, I was ready enough to camp here hoping to take the ships. But now I am afraid of Achilles. He will not let us keep the battle down on the plain but will fight for our city and our wives. Let us go back to the city, for this is how it will be. If he finds us here in the morning, we will know what he is only too well. And we will be glad enough to get back to sacred Troy, those of us who escape. If we do as I say, we will keep our strength up in the city guarded by its walls and high gates. In the morning we will take our stand on the walls, and it will be the worse for him if he comes to fight us there."

Then with an angry glance Hector answered: "Polydamas, this is no longer to my pleasure. Have you not had enough of being inside those walls? In the old days the riches of Priam's city were on all men's lips, but now our treasures are wasted out of our houses and sold away to Phrygia and Maeonia. So now, when the son of crooked-counseling Cronos has given me glory at the ships, let us have no more of such fool's counsel here. Not a man of the Trojans will hear you. I will not let them. No, these are my orders. Take your supper by companies, keep a good watch, and be ready every man. In the morning, at the coming of Dawn, let us fight on for the ships. And if Achilles will come out to fight, so much the worse for him. I will stand against him face to face, to see if he can win glory or I. The god of war is the same to all and a killer of him that would kill."

So Hector said, and the foolish Trojans shouted loudly, for Pallas Athene took their senses from them. They were for Hector and his bad counsel and against Polydamas though his words were wise. So they took their supper. But all night through the Greeks sorrowed loudly for Patroclus. And Achilles first cried out among them. He put his man-killing hands on Patroclus' breast with many moans and said: "Alas! Useless were my words to Menoetius in our house. I told him I would bring his brave son back from the wasting of Troy, with his part of its treasures. But Zeus does not give their hearts' desire to all men. We two are both fated to make the same earth of Troyland red with our blood. No more than you will I be welcomed back by Peleus to his house or by my mother Thetis. But seeing that quickly now I come after you under earth, I will not give you to the fire till I have Hector's head and armor; and I will cut the throats of twelve sons of the Trojans here and put them with you on the fire. But till then by these ships day and night about you deep-breasted women of Troyland will sorrow in tears—women you and I took by the power of our long spears." And he washed the body and put it on a bed and covered it from head to foot with a soft linen cloth.

Now silver-footed Thetis came to the house of Hephaestus, fairest of the houses of Heaven, made all of bronze, which the crook-footed god had built for himself. She found him sweating and hard at work making three-legged ves-

sels, twenty of them, to stand by the wall of his house. He
had put gold wheels under them so that they could roll of
themselves into the meetings of the gods and go back again
to his house, at his orders; wonderful they were to see. They
were ready, but he had not put their ears to them and this
he was doing. And bright-veiled Charis, his wife, came for-
ward and took Thetis' hand and said: "What brings you
here to our house, Thetis, honored and ever welcome? You
have not been here for a long time. Come and let me get you
something." And she put her in a beautiful silver-worked
seat with a footstool for the feet and cried to Hephaestus:
"Hephaestus, come here. Thetis wants you." And the
strong-armed god answered: "Truly a dread and honored
goddess is in my house, she who saved me when I was in
pain from that great fall my shameless mother gave me, hop-
ing to put me away because of my crooked foot. Eurynome
and Thetis took good care of me then down under the waters
of Oceanus. So now is the time to pay fair-haired Thetis the
full price for saving me. Give her the best we have while I put
my work on one side."

He got up, the great hard-breathing mass of him, uneven
in his walk, but the thin legs under him still were quick.
And he turned the bellows from the fire and put all the
tools he was working with in a great silver chest, and took
a sponge and wiped his hands and face and his great neck
and hairy breast, and put on a shirt and took up a thick staff,
and went out on his crooked foot; but handmaids of ham-
mered gold who looked like living girls came forward to
support their maker. There is understanding in their hearts,
and speech and strength, and they are good at handiwork

by the gift of the immortal gods. They helped their lord and he walked, unevenly, to where Thetis was and seated himself and took her hand, saying: "Welcome, Thetis. Now tell me what you want. I will do it for you, if I can, and if it can be done at all."

Thetis answered him, in tears: "Hephaestus, is there a goddess in Olympus on whom Zeus has put sorrows like mine? Me only of the sea's daughters he gave to a mortal in marriage, to Peleus, son of Aeacus, and I have been his wife much against my will. And now he is old and keeps to his house and I have other sorrows. He gave me a son and I brought him up, a hero of heroes. I sent him in the ships to war with the Trojans and now I will never welcome him back home to Peleus' house. And while he is still alive in the sunlight, he is sorrowing, and though I go to him I cannot help him. The girl the Greeks gave him as a prize, Agamemnon has taken back from his very arms. He was wasting his heart out sorrowing for her, while the Trojans were holding the Greeks at the sterns of their ships. And the old men of the Greeks prayed him for help, naming many glorious gifts. But he would not save them himself. He sent Patroclus out and put his own armor on him, and with him went the Myrmidons. And they fought about the Scaean gates all day and would have taken and wasted the city, but Apollo killed Menoetius' son and gave glory to Hector. That is why I have come to you. Will you give my son, whose end is so near, a shield and armor? For what he had was taken from Patroclus by the Trojans; and now my son lies stretched on the earth in his sorrow."

And the great artist of the two strong arms answered:

"Take heart and do not let it trouble you any more. If only I could keep him from death when his hour comes! But certainly I can make him armor at which all who see it will wonder."

Saying this, he went to his bellows and turned them toward the fire and told them to work. And the twenty bellows blew upon the vessels as Hephaestus desired and his work needed. And he put strong bronze and tin with gold and silver over the fire. Then he placed his great anvil on its stand and took his great hammer in one hand and the tongs in the other.

First he made a shield, great and strong, every part with a design upon it, and put around it a bright, threefold ring.

On the shield itself he put the earth, the heavens, the sea and the untiring sun, and the moon at the full, and all the stars which are the crown of Heaven: the Pleiades, the Hyades, and great Orion, and the Bear, that men sometimes name the Wain, that turns always in her place facing Orion and has no part in the baths of Ocean.

And he put there two fair cities of mortal men. In one there were marriages and feastings, and in the light of flaming torches they were taking brides through the city, singing the bride song loudly. Young men were whirling in the dance and the music sounded on, and the women stood before their doors to watch. The people had come together, too, in the meeting place, for two men were arguing there about the blood price for a man who had been killed; one said he had paid it in full, but the other would take nothing and both were looking for a decision from a judge. And the people were supporting both, taking sides. And heralds kept order while the old men sat on polished seats of stone in the sacred circle, ready to stand and give judgment each in turn. And before them were two talents of gold, for him whose judgment was the best.

But around the other city were two armies. And two counsels they had in mind: to waste the town or to make a division of all the fair city held. But the townspeople were not giving up, but were arming for an ambush. On the wall stood their dear wives and young children and the old men with them. But the rest went out with Ares and Pallas Athene, made in gold, at their head. Fair and tall in their armor they were, and looked like gods, while the men at their feet were smaller. And when they came to the place for the ambush, in a river bed where there was a watering place for the herds, they sat down clothed in bright bronze. And two men were put to keep watch for the coming of the sheep and cattle. And they came and with them two herdsmen playing on pipes, with no thought of the ambush. Then the others, when they saw them, ran quickly and cut off the sheep and cattle and killed the herdsmen. But the armies before the city, when they heard the noise, got into their chariots and came up quickly. Then they fought by the river banks, and hit one another with bronze-pointed spears. As living mortals they joined in battle, dragging away the bodies of the killed.

And he put there, too, a soft new-plowed field, rich and wide. And many plowmen were wheeling their oxen, working them up and down. And when, after turning they came to the headland of the field, a man would step forward and give each a cup of honey-sweet wine; and the plowmen turned in the field to come back to the headland again. The field looked black after their plowing, though made of gold. So wonderful was the work.

And he put there, too, a king's wheat field, and his men were cutting the wheat with sharp sickles in their hands. Armfuls were falling to the earth, while others were taking them up and putting them together with bands of twisted straw. And near them the king was standing in silence, his heart full of joy. Others under an oak were making a feast ready, a great ox that was their offering; and the women threw barley on the meat for the workers' midday meal.

He put there, too, a fair vineyard, made of gold; the grapes were black and the vines were held up on silver stakes. And round it was a ditch of dark metal and outside that a wall of tin. There was only one path to it by which they came and went when they took the grapes. And young girls and boys were joyfully taking the honey-sweet fruit in baskets. Among them a boy made music on his lyre and sang the Linos-song in his delicate voice. And the others kept time with him, their feet falling together.

He put there, too, a herd of straight-horned cattle. They were made of gold and tin, and they came out to feed by the sounding river in the waving grass. And four herdsmen walked with them, made in gold, and nine swift-footed dogs came after. But two dread lions were holding a bellowing bull and the dogs and young men ran at them. The lions were biting through the bull's skin and drinking its black blood; but the herdsmen could do nothing but urge on the dogs and these were afraid and stood by barking and springing away.

And the strong-armed god put there a fair mountain slope, with many white-wooled sheep feeding, and sheepfolds and roofed huts.

There, too, he made a dancing place like that which Daedalus made of old for fair Ariadne. There young men were dancing and girls you would give many cattle for, with their hands on one another's forearms. The girls were in fair linen, the young men in shirts, well made and lightly oiled. The girls were crowned with leaves and the young men had knives of gold hanging from silver cords. Sometimes they would dance in a ring, as a potter will sit with his wheel between his hands seeing if it will run; sometimes they would step in lines to meet each other. And a great company stood round in joy, while two tumblers whirled in the middle giving the measure.

Round the outermost edge of the shield he put the great power of the river Oceanus.

When he had made the shield so great and strong, he made a breastplate brighter than fire and a great helmet, richly worked with a crest of gold; and he made him leg guards of tin.

When the glorious god of the two strong arms had made all the armor, he took it and put it before Achilles' mother. Then she sprang down from snowy Olympus with it.

19

IN THE morning Thetis came to the ships with the gifts
of Hephaestus. And she found Achilles sorrowing aloud
with Patroclus' body in his arms, and about him his
friends were in tears. The bright goddess came to his
side and took his hand, saying: "My child, we must let this
man be, for all our pain, seeing that he is dead by the will
of the gods. But here, from Hephaestus, is armor, very
beautiful and such as no man ever had before." And she put
the arms down before Achilles and they rang loudly in
their glory. Then all the Myrmidons shook with fear, and
no man had the courage to look at them. But when Achilles
saw them, rage for battle came on him again and his eyes
burned like flame; and he was glad as he held up the gifts

of the god. But when he had taken his joy in looking at their glory, he said to his mother: "I will arm now for battle. But while I am away I am afraid that flies will get at Patroclus' wounds." And the goddess answered: "Have no fear, my child. I will take that upon me. But do you bring the Greek chiefs together and unsay your anger against Agamemnon. Then arm for battle and put on all your strength."

And she made him full of unshakable courage, and on Patroclus she dropped ambrosia and red nectar so that his body would undergo no change.

Then by the side of the sea Achilles went shouting loudly to the Greeks. They came—even the shipmen and keepers of the stores came now—to the place of meeting, happy because Achilles was coming back into the war. Among them came two who were wounded—Diomede and Odysseus—helping themselves with their spears and they sat in front of the meeting. Last of all came Agamemnon, wounded, too.

When they were all together, Achilles stood and said: "How was it better for us, Agamemnon, for you and for me, to rage in such high anger about a girl? Why did not Artemis kill her among the ships with an arrow on the day that I took her at Lernessus? Fewer Greeks then would have been killed by the Trojans through the heat of my anger. But these things we will let be, for all our pain, quieting the hearts in our breasts because we must. Come now into the field once more. Let us see if the Trojans now have a mind to sleep by our ships or not."

The Greeks grew happy because Achilles had put away his anger. And Agamemnon, chief of chiefs, said from where he sat: "Friends, Greeks, fighters, take good note of all I say. It was not I who am to blame—but Zeus and Fate and Erinys that walks in the dark. Here in the place of meeting they made me blind on the day when I took his prize of honor from Achilles. What could I do? All things are in the hand of God. First daughter of Zeus is Ate, who blinds us all. Her delicate feet do not walk on earth but over the heads of men as she makes them fall; and this one or that she chains. Even Zeus she blinded at one time, though they say he is the greatest among gods and men. But because I was blinded and Zeus took my mind from me, now I am ready to give you, Achilles, all that Odysseus offered you before, when he went to your hut. Withhold you a while from battle and see if my gifts are enough."

But Achilles answered: "Great Agamemnon, chief of chiefs, as to these gifts, to give them if you will, as is right, or keep them back, rests with you. But this is no time for talk. There is a great work to be done. To arms. Let each man as he fights think that Achilles is with him again."

But Odysseus took men and went to Agamemnon's hut and what had been said was done. Seven tripods and twenty bright cauldrons and twelve horses they brought out and seven women skillful in handiwork—and the eighth was fair-faced Briseis. And all these and the ten talents of gold they took to Achilles' hut. But Briseis—beautiful as golden Aphrodite—when she saw Patroclus dead threw herself upon him crying aloud, and with her two hands she scratched her breast and soft neck and beautiful face. Beautiful as a goddess, she said: "Patroclus, friend to my unhappy heart. You were living when I went from this hut and now I find you dead. So evil comes on me after evil. My husband, to whom my father and queenly mother gave me, I saw cut down before our city, and my three dear brothers with him. But when swift Achilles killed my husband and wasted the city of godlike Mynes, you would have stopped my tears. You said you would make me Achilles' wife and that he would take me in his ships to Phthia to a marriage feast among the Myrmidons. Endlessly I cry aloud for your death, for you were ever kind." And the other women added their cries. For Patroclus truly they cried, but each for her own sorrows too.

Then the Greeks poured out from the swift ships; and with them from the ships came arms and armor, thick and swift as snow blown past by the North Wind, cold offspring of bright Heaven. And all earth laughed with the sunlight on the bronze and the sound of men's feet. Among them Achilles made himself ready for battle.

His teeth were tight together and his eyes like flames of fire, so great was the pain in his heart. In such anger against the Trojans he put on the armor Hephaestus had made him. First on his legs he put the guards and then the breastplate about his chest. From his shoulders he hung the bronze sword ornamented with silver and then took up the shield so great and strong. Bright like the moon it looked from afar. As a light seen by sailors from out at sea, when a fire is burning high up by a lonely hut in the mountains—but stormwinds against their will take them away from their friends—so seemed the light of Achilles' shield. And on his head he put the fear-awaking helmet—like a star it was, the horsehair crested helmet, and the gold feathers Hephaestus had added waved about the crest. And Achilles tested it all and moved freely within it—like wings it lifted him up. And from its stand he took his father's spear that Cheiron had given to Peleus. And Automedon made ready the horses and sprang upon the chariot. Then terribly Achilles cried to the horses: "Xanthus and Balius, offspring of Podarge, bring your driver safely back, this time, when we have ended our fighting. Do not to him as you did to Patroclus."

Then swift Xanthus answered—for Hera gave him words. Suddenly he bent his head and his long hair touched the earth. "Dread Achilles," he said, "we will save you now, but your day of death is near. And we will not be the cause, but a strong god and overpowering Fate. It was not through any wrongdoing of ours that Patroclus fell, but the best of the gods, fair-haired Leto's son, killed him among the fighters, giving glory to Hector. Though we ran with the West Wind, swiftest, men say, of all winds, still it is your fate to be killed in battle by a god and a man."

When he had said so much, Erinyes stopped his voice. Achilles, greatly moved, answered: "Xanthus, why do you tell me of my death? Well I know that I am to die here, far from my dear father and my mother, but not before I have given the Trojans more than enough of fighting."

Then, with a cry he drove his immortal horses forward.

20

༒༒༒༒༒༒༒༒༒༒༒༒༒༒༒༒༒༒༒༒༒༒༒༒༒༒༒༒༒༒༒༒༒༒༒༒༒༒
༒༒༒༒༒༒༒༒༒༒༒༒༒༒༒༒༒༒༒༒༒༒༒༒༒༒༒༒༒༒༒༒༒༒༒༒༒༒

SO HE went into the fighting. And the gods joined
in on one side or the other. Zeus, father of gods and
men, thundered from on high and Poseidon made
the earth and the mountaintops themselves shake.
And then to many of the Trojan fighters did Achilles give
their death as he sprang among them, his heart clothed with
power, crying his fearful cry. And Hector's young brother
Polydorus was one of them. His father Priam would never
let him fight though he was the swiftest-footed of all the
Trojans. He was the youngest and the dearest of all his sons
to old Priam. And here he was in the front of the battle,
the foolish boy, letting everybody see how swiftly he could

run, till Achilles took him with his spear point as he ran by. Through him went the spear and he fell to his knees moaning and a dark cloud came over him as he held his bowels to him with his hands.

When Hector saw his young brother so, his eyes were misted over and he went up against Achilles like a flame of fire, balancing his sharp spear. And Achilles saw him and sprang up and cried: "There! There is the man who pierced me to the heart in killing my friend." And angrily he looked on Hector and said: "Come near—to meet your Fate the quicker."

But with no touch of fear, Hector of the flashing helmet answered: "Son of Peleus, do not think you can make me afraid with words, like a child. I, too, have words to say or keep unsaid. I know that you are stronger far than I. But these things are on the knees of the gods. For my spear, too, has been found to be sharp before now."

And he threw his spear, but with a light breath Athene turned it from Achilles and it came back to Hector falling there at his feet. Then Achilles sprang upon him to kill him. But Apollo, as a god may, took Hector up, covering him in mist. And three times Achilles sprang upon him with his spear of bronze and three times cut only the mist. Then he cried: "Dog, once again you have escaped death, near though it was to you. Apollo has saved you again. You must pray to him hard when you go among the whirling spears. But I will make an end of you still, if any god will help me."

And he killed many and many another Trojan. As when a forest fire is burning through the hollows of a sun-dried mountainside and the wind drives great tongues of flame in every direction, so Achilles with his spear, like some god, went raging through the Trojans—and the black earth ran with blood.

21

AND ACHILLES cut the armies of the Trojans in two. One part he sent running back to Troy; and the other part, like locusts before a grass fire flying into water, came to the banks of the deep river Xanthus and threw themselves in and the banks rang with their shouting as they went swimming this way and that, whirled about in the eddies. And the hero put his spear on one side against a tree and went into the river with his sword only. And when his arms were tired with killing, he took twelve young men living out of the river to be a blood price for dead Patroclus. These he took out, helpless as fawns, and gave them to his men to be taken back to the ships.

And then he came upon a son of Priam, Lycaon, as he was escaping out of the water. Once before Achilles had taken him, finding him one night in Priam's orchard. He was cutting young branches there from a fig tree to make the sides of a chariot. And Achilles had taken him prisoner and sold him oversea; and at last Lycaon had got away in secret and come back to Troy to the house of his fathers. For eleven days he was happy there among his friends again. But on the twelfth some god threw him once more into the hands of Achilles, who was to send him now to the house of Hades, much against his will. He was unarmed when Achilles saw him, without spear or sword or shield, and his tired knees were giving way under him as he came up the bank.

Then, deeply moved, Achilles said to himself in his wonder: "What is this? If this man can come back so, will the greathearted Trojans I have killed come back living from the underworld? Could not the deep of the gray sea keep him away, which holds many against their will? Let him taste now of my spear point. Let me know if the life-giving earth will hold him down who holds down even the strong."

So he thought and waited. But Lycaon came near to touch Achilles' knees in prayer. Achilles lifted high his spear but Lycaon ran in under it and prayed him with one hand on Achilles' knees and the other on the spear, and with words feathered like an arrow he prayed to him: "Have pity on me, Achilles, for my prayers to you are sacred. At your table I tasted the grain of Demeter after you took me prisoner in the well-ordered orchard, before you sold me oversea for the price of a hundred oxen. Three times as much

I paid to get free. I have been home again in Troy only twelve days and now cruel fate has put me in your hands once more. Father Zeus must hate me. To a short life my mother bore me. My brother Polydorus you killed but now. Hear me out and do not kill me. My mother was not Hector's mother. I am only the half-brother of the man who killed your friend."

So he prayed, but pitiless was the voice he heard. "Fool, offer me no such words. Till Patroclus fell, it was my pleasure to have pity on the Trojans and many of them I took and sold oversea. But now, not one of them may escape death, least of all any of the sons of Priam. No, friend, you die with them. Why do you sorrow so? Patroclus died, who was better far than you. And do you not see what sort of man I am—how beautiful and tall? A good man was my father and a goddess mother bore me. But over me, too, hang death and fate. There will come a dawn or eve or midday when some man will take my life in battle—with the spear or an arrow from the string."

So he said and the other's knees were loosed where he was and he let go the spear and bent his head with his arms outstretched. But Achilles hit him on the collarbone by the neck and all the two-edged sword went in and the dark blood wetted the earth. And Achilles took Lycaon by the foot and threw him into the river to go his way.

The old man Priam stood on the Heaven-built wall and saw Achilles driving the Trojans before him in flight and there was no help to be had. So he went down crying aloud and told the gatekeepers to undo the gates and open them wide and let the Trojans in. And they had no more courage to wait for one another outside the city to know who had escaped or who had been killed in the fighting, but all whose knees and feet could save them poured through the gates.

22

SO THROUGHOUT the city, like helpless fawns, the Trojans were wiping the sweat off them and drinking to wet their dry throats, as they rested on the fair crest of the walls, while the Greeks, with their shields on their shoulders, came toward the city. But deadly fate held Hector where he was in front of the Scaean gates.

Then Achilles turned toward Troy. Swift, as a prize-winning chariot horse running all out across the plain, so swift were Achilles' feet and knees. And the old man, Priam, was the first to see him coming. And to Priam he seemed like the star which comes out at harvest time—bright are his rays among the armies of dark night—the star men name the Dog of Orion. Brightest of all, he is but a sign of evil. Even so the bronze flashed on Achilles' breast as he ran. And the old man moaned, and took his head in his hands and cried to Hector, his son, who was standing before the gates ready to fight with Achilles: "Hector, dear son, do not wait there by yourself for Achilles. He is stronger far than you. Would that the gods loved him as I do. He would quickly enough be food for dogs and birds then. How many of my sons has he killed or sold to the islands oversea, and now I cannot see Polydorus or Lycaon among the Trojans who came back into the city! Come in, come inside the walls, my son! Save the Trojans, and have pity on me! It is not so bad for a young man's body to be seen naked, wounded by the sharp bronze—but for an old man when he is dead to be torn by dogs in full view, that is the worst thing which can come to man."

So he cried pulling at his white hair, but Hector was not to be won over. And his mother Hecuba cried to him, too. "Hector, respect me and pity me if ever I gave you the breast. Fight with Achilles from inside the walls. Do not stand there to face him. Cruel he is and if he kills you I will never have you before me on a bed to sorrow over, dear offshoot of myself, nor will your wife, but he will give you to his dogs far away from us by the Greek ships."

But Hector would not hear them as he waited there for Achilles. And deeply moved, he said to himself: "Alas, if I go inside the gates Polydamas will be the first to say that this is my doing. For he told me to bring the Trojans into the city that terrible night, when Achilles came out. But

I would not hear him—how much better if I had! But now that I have brought destruction on us all, blind fool that I was, I cannot face the Trojans and their wives. Some worse man may say: 'Hector, believing too much in himself, undid us all.' They will say that. It will be far better to meet Achilles man to man and kill him and then go in; or be killed by him, in all honor, before the city. Or how would it be to put down my shield and helmet and rest my spear against the wall and go to meet unmatched Achilles and tell him we will give up Helen, and with her all the treasure Paris took from Menelaus, and give the Greeks half of all we have as well? But why do I argue with myself like this? Achilles would have no pity on me but would kill me right away as though I were a woman, if I were unarmed. This is no time for boy and girl talk with him—boy and girl talk under some rock or oak tree. Better fight at once and see on whose side Zeus will be."

As he thought so, Achilles came near in his waving helmet, with his great Pelean spear lifted; and suddenly fear moved Hector and away from the gates under the walls of Troy he ran, with swift-footed Achilles after him. Past the lookout station, and by the wind-waved fig tree away from the wall by the wagon road they went, and past the two springs which feed eddying Xanthus. One runs with warm water and a smoke goes up from it as if from a fire, the other even in summer is cold as snow or ice. And near them are the wide stone basins where the wives and daughters of the Trojans washed their clothes of old in the time of peace, before the Greeks came to Troyland. By these they ran

—a good man in front but a far stronger man at his heels. And the prize they ran for was no bull's skin, or common prize for the swift-footed, but the life of horse-taming Hector.

And all the gods looked on. Then the father of gods and men said: "My heart sorrows for Hector, who has burned many thighs of oxen on the crests of Ida and in the city. Now think and take counsel, gods. Are we to save him from death or now at last kill him, a good man though he is, at Achilles' hands?"

Then the goddess, flashing-eyed Athene, said: "Father, Lord of the bright lightning and the dark cloud, what are you saying? Would you save from death a mortal man whose hour has long been fixed by fate? Do as you will, but know that we other gods are not all with you in this."

And in answer Zeus said: "Take heart, my child. I am not as serious as I seem. Do as your pleasure is and hold back no longer." And down from Olympus Athene went.

Three times round Troy Hector and Achilles ran. Whenever Hector made for the Dardanian gates to the cover of the walls, where the Trojans could help him by throwing, Achilles would head him off and turn him back toward the plain, keeping on the city side. They ran as in a dream where one man cannot escape or overtake another. And how could Hector have escaped so far, if Apollo, for the last time, had not kept up his strength and made swift his knees? And Achilles signed to the other Greeks not to throw their spears at Hector. Three times round Troy they went, but when they came the fourth time to the springs, Zeus lifted up his golden balance and Hector's fate went down; and Phoebus Apollo left him.

Then Athene came to Achilles and said: "Stand and take breath while I go and make Hector fight with you man to man." And Achilles did so, resting on his great spear. And Athene went to Hector, putting on the form and voice of Deïphobus, his brother.

"Dear brother," she said, "now let us two meet Achilles' attack together." And Hector answered: "Deïphobus, you were always dearest to me of my brothers, but now I honor you in my heart even more. You, only, have had the courage to come out here to help me while the others stay inside."

And bright-eyed Athene said: "Truly, my brother, they did all they could, with their prayers, to keep me back— so much they fear Achilles—but now let us fight."

With such words Athene tricked him; and Hector, coming near to Achilles, said: "I will run from you no longer, Achilles, but kill you now or be killed. And let this be our agreement before all the gods as witnesses: if Zeus lets me outlive you and take your life, I will give your body back to the Greeks, after taking your armor. And you will do the same."

But with an angry look Achilles answered: "Talk not to me of agreements, Hector. Between lions and men there is no swearing of oaths. How can wolves and sheep be of one mind? They must hate one another all through. No more of this, but fight your best. For now Pallas Athene will overcome you by my spear. Now you must pay for all my sorrows for my friends you have killed."

He lifted his far-shadowing spear as he spoke and threw. Hector watched its coming and bent low so that it went over him and fixed itself in the earth. But Athene took it out and gave it back to Achilles without Hector's seeing her. And Hector cried: "So you did not know from Zeus the hour of my death, O godlike Achilles! Did you think your false tongue would make me afraid? Now escape my spear if you can."

And he lifted his far-shadowing spear and threw it and hit Achilles' shield, but the shield turned it back. And Hector saw and cried to Deïphobus loudly for a long spear. But there was no man there. Then Hector knew all in his heart and said: "Alas! Now they have brought me to my death. I thought Deïphobus was with me, but he is inside the walls and that was Athene who tricked me. Now death is very near me and there is no way of escape. This from of old was the pleasure of Zeus and his son, Apollo, who helped me before, but now my fate has come upon me. At least let me die fighting, to be honored by later men who hear of this."

And he took his sharp sword that hung by his side, a great sword and strong, and sprang on Achilles like an eagle which falls from a cloud on some lamb or hare. But Achilles ran upon him, his heart raging, his breast covered by his shield and the gold feathers on his four-horned helmet waving. As a star comes out among the stars of night, the star of evening, the most beautiful of the stars of heaven, even so came the light from the bronze of his spear as he lifted it in his right hand looking for the place most open for the blow. Now Hector's body was covered with bronze armor, the beautiful armor he had taken from great Patroclus when he killed him; but there was an opening where the collarbones come into the neck; and there, as he came on, Achilles let drive with his spear and straight through the neck went the point. But the bronze-weighted spear did not cut the windpipe, so that Hector still had his voice. Then as he fell in the dust, Achilles gloried over him: "You thought, Hector, you would be safe when you took that armor from Patroclus. Little you thought, you fool, of me, far away among my ships. But now, stronger far, I have come from them and loosed your knees. The Greeks will give him his funeral but throw you to the dogs and birds."

Then Hector, as the breath went from him, prayed: "By your life and knees and parents take the bronze and gold and all the gifts my father and mother will offer you and send my body back so that the Trojans and the Trojans' wives may give me to the fire after my death."

But with an angry look Achilles answered: "Pray me not, dog, by knees or parents. O that I could make myself cut up your flesh and eat it raw myself, for what you have done. There is no man living who can keep the dogs from your head, Hector—no, not though they paid me your weight in gold."

And dying Hector answered: "I know you for what you are, and knew it before; the heart in your breast is of iron. See that I do not bring the anger of the gods down upon you on the day when Paris and Apollo kill you, strong though you are, at the Scaean gate."

He ended and death overtook him and his spirit went

from him down to the house of Hades, crying out sadly against its fate. And after his death Achilles said to him: "Lie dead there; I am ready for my own death whenever Zeus and the other immortals send it."

He pulled his spear out and put it aside and took the armor from Hector's body. And the other Greeks ran up to wonder at Hector's beauty. And all who came near wounded him with their spears. And one would say looking at another: "Hector is softer now to handle than when he burned the ships with fire." And when Achilles had taken off the armor, he stood and said to the Greeks: "Let us see what the Trojans are minded to do now that the gods have let us overcome this man who has done us more damage than all the rest together. But what am I thinking of? Patroclus still waits at the ships for his funeral. How can I forget him while I live on and my knees are quick! Even if in the house of Hades dead men forget their friends, even there I will not forget him. But come, sons of the Greeks, let us go back to the ships singing our song of glory and taking this man with us. For we have won great glory. We have killed highborn Hector to whom the Trojans throughout their city prayed as to a god."

And he cut the backs of Hector's heels and put cords of leather through and tied them to his chariot. He lifted in the armor and got in and touched the horses with his whip. Swiftly they started forward. The dust went up round Hector's dark hair outstretched and his head that was so beautiful before; for now Zeus had given him over to be shamefully handled in his own land where he was born.

Andromache, Hector's wife, knew nothing of these things. No one had come to tell her that her husband was still outside the gates. She was working on a great purple cloth in the innermost part of her house, threading into it flowers of many colors. And she told her fair-haired hand-maids to put a great vessel, a tripod, on the fire, for a hot bath to be ready for Hector when he came back from the fighting. She did not know that far from all baths Athene had overthrown him by the hand of Achilles. Then she heard loud cries and moans from the wall and she was shaken and the needle fell from her hand. And to her hand-maids she said: "Two of you, come with me and let us see what it is. It was Hecuba's voice I heard. I am afraid Achilles may have cut off Hector from the city."

So saying she went quickly out and onto the wall. There she stopped and looked, and saw him as he was dragged before the city. The swift horses were dragging him toward the Greek ships. Then dark night came down on her and she fell backward breathing out her spirit. From her head fell her headdress and the veil that golden Aphrodite had given her on the day that Hector took her as his bride from Eëtion's house after bringing bride gifts unnumbered. Her husband's sisters and his brothers' wives came round her and supported her, for she was near to death in her trouble. Then she breathed again. And she came to herself and lifted up her voice in sorrow among the women of Troy, saying: "Ah, Hector, to one fate we were born, you in Troy in the house of Priam and I in Thebe under wooded Placus in the house of Eëtion, ill-fated father of a cruel-

fated child! Would that he had never begotten me. You
go now into the house of Hades under earth and you leave
me, in bitter sorrow, a widow in your house. And our
son is a child. You can do nothing now for him, Hector, nor
he for you. If he escapes from this war, still trouble and sor-
row will be his, for other men will take your lands. A child
is cut off from his friends on the day his father dies; his head is
bent low and his face is wet with tears. In his need he goes
to his father's friends; he takes one by the coat and pulls
at the shirt of another. And of those who are moved with
pity, one holds out a small cup to his mouth for a little; his lips
he wets but his mouth is not made wet. And some child with a
living father and mother pushes him away from the feast with
blows saying: 'Out with you! No father of yours is at our
table.' Then he goes back in tears to his mother—Astyanax,
who ate only marrow and the rich fat of sheep on his father's
knee; and when he had played till he was tired, he would
sleep in his nurse's arms in a soft bed; but now that he has
no father, evil days come on him, my poor Astyanax. The
Trojans gave him that name because only you guarded their
gates and their long walls. But now by the ships, far from
your parents, worms will eat you when the dogs have ended.
Naked you will lie, though here in your house are stores
of linen, delicate, fair, made by the hands of women. But
I will burn all this—no profit to you who will not lie in it—
to be honor to you from the men and the women of Troy."

So she said in her sorrowing, and the women joined their
cry.

23

SO THROUGHOUT the city they sorrowed. But the Greeks when they came to the sea went each to his own ship. Only Achilles kept his Myrmidons together, saying: "Let us not undo the horses, but with the chariots go near and sorrow for Patroclus, for this does rightful honor to the dead. When we have had full comfort in our sorrowing, we will undo our horses and take food."

Then, crying in one voice with Achilles, they drove three times round Patroclus' body; and Thetis moved in them the desire to sorrow. The sands and their armor were wet with their tears, so great a lord of fear they sorrowed for. And Achilles put his man-killing hands on Patroclus' breast and said: "Be it well with you, Patroclus, even in the house of Hades. Now I am doing all that I told you I would do: that I would drag Hector here and give him raw to the dogs to eat, and cut the throats of twelve glorious sons of the Trojans before your pyre."

And he gave shameful treatment to Hector, stretching him on his face in the dust before Patroclus. Then he made for his Myrmidons a funeral feast to comfort their hearts, till everywhere about the body the blood of bulls, pigs and sheep ran cup-deep.

But Agamemnon sent the chiefs to bring Achilles to his hut. And there the clear-voiced heralds were to heat water in a great vessel for him to wash off the blood from his wounds. But he would not, and swore an oath: "By Zeus, highest and best of gods, no water may come near my head till I have given Patroclus to the fire and built him a mound, and shaved my hair, for no second sorrow will pierce my heart while I live. But for this hour let us give way to the hateful feast. In the morning, king of men, Agamemnon, order the people to bring wood and make ready everything a dead man must have when he goes into the misty dark, so that untiring fire may burn him out of sight and the army turn to its work again."

So they did. And when they had put from them the desire of food and drink, the others went each man to his hut to take his rest. But Achilles lay moaning among his Myrmidons by the side of the sounding sea, in an open place where the waves washed in. And a deep sleep came upon him, loosing the cares of his heart, for very tired he was, with running

after Hector round windy Troy. And then came to him
the spirit of Patroclus, in all things like his living self, in
form and fair eyes and voice, and he was clothed as in life.
He stood at Achilles' head and said: "You sleep, and have
no more thought for me, Achilles. Not in my life were you
unmindful of me; but now in my death! Give me to the fire
now swiftly so that I may go in through the gates of Hades.
Far off the spirits keep me, shades of men who have no
more to do, and will not let me join them across the River.
And give me now your hand in your pity, for I never will
come again from Hades after you have given me my right-
ful fire. Never will we sit by ourselves in counsel again, for
hateful fate has me, the fate that was mine from birth. You,
too, godlike Achilles, are fated to be brought low under the
walls of Troy. And hear now, if you will, my request. Do
not separate my bones from yours, Achilles; let them lie
together as we were brought up together in your house.
Menoetius brought me as a little boy to your country be-
cause I had killed Amphidamus' son, but not on purpose, in
anger over the dice. Then your father took me into his house
to be your companion-in-arms; so now let our bones lie in
one urn, a golden urn, two-handled, which your mother
gave you."

And Achilles answered: "Why, my brother, do you
come to tell me all this? I will do all. But stand nearer and,
though it is but for a little, let us throw our arms about one
another and give full way to our sorrow." He stretched out
his hands but felt him not, for the spirit, like a mist, went
under earth, feebly moaning.

Then Achilles sprang up in wonder and hit his hands to-
gether, crying: "See you, even in the house of Hades, the
spirit or shade is something—though the life is not in it.
For all night long the spirit of Patroclus has stood over me,
moaning and telling me what to do, and he was wonder-
fully like his living self."

And in them all he moved a desire to sorrow aloud. Rose-
fingered Dawn found them still crying out round the body.
Then Agamemnon sent men with mules to get wood and
they took axes for cutting down the trees and strong cords,
and the mules went in front. Up and down and sideways and
across at all angles they went. When they came to the slopes
of many-springed Ida, they worked hard cutting down high-
crested oaks with the long-edged bronze. With a noise like
thunder the trees kept falling. Then they dragged them
down and the mules cut up the earth with their feet as they
pushed through the thick undergrowth. All the woodcut-
ters carried logs on their shoulders and threw them down,
man after man, at the place by the sea where Achilles would
make a great mound for Patroclus and himself. And when
they had got in the wood they sat down there together. But
Achilles ordered the Myrmidons to put on their armor and
make their chariots ready. The chariots went first and a
cloud of footmen after. In the middle his brothers-in-arms
carried Patroclus. They covered him over with the hair
they cut from their heads and threw on the body. And
Achilles held up Patroclus' head, sorrowing; for like no other
was the man he was helping into the house of Hades.

When they came to the place they put the body down

and built up the wood. Then Achilles cut off the yellow hair that he had been keeping for the river Spercheüs. And looking out over the wine-dark sea, greatly moved, he said: "Spercheüs, to no purpose my father swore that when I came home I would cut off my hair and make a sacred offering to your waters. He swore it, but you did not give him his desire. Now seeing that I am not to go home to my own country, I give this hair to Patroclus to take with him."

Then he put the hair in Patroclus' hands and all were moved to sorrow. The light of the sun would have gone down upon their sorrowing if Achilles had not come to Agamemnon and said: "Let the army go and make ready their meal now. But let the chiefs stay; we to whom Patroclus is dearest will see to what is needed here."

Then Agamemnon sent the men back to their ships and Achilles with Patroclus' nearest friends built up the wood and made a pyre a hundred feet each way and on the top of it, with sorrowing hearts, they placed the dead man. And many sheep and cattle they killed and skinned before the pyre. And from them Achilles took the fat and covered the dead with it from head to foot, and put the skinned bodies about him; and two-handled jars of honey and oil he placed by the bed. Then he threw four strong horses upon the pyre, moaning as he did so. And he cut the throats of two of the nine house dogs Patroclus kept and threw them on the pyre. Then he killed the twelve brave sons of the Trojans with his sword—evil work of his heart's designing. And he put to it the iron power of fire to feed on all. Then moaning he cried: "Be it well with you, Patroclus, even in the house of Hades.

For now I am doing all that I said. Twelve brave sons of the Trojans, on all these with you the fire is feeding. But Hector, the son of Priam, I do not give to the fire but to dogs."

But no dogs could come near Hector, for Aphrodite kept them from him day and night and she put oil on him, ambrosial oil of roses, so that his body would take no scratch when Achilles dragged it.

But the pyre of Patroclus did not take fire. Then Achilles prayed to the North Wind and to the West Wind. And Iris took his prayer to the house of the West Wind where all the winds were feasting. And swiftly they came, driving the clouds before them, and blew on the seas and the waves swelled under their breath; and they came to deep-soiled Troyland and fell upon the pyre. Loud then roared the flames. All night long they blew upon the flames of the pyre; and all night long Achilles with a two-handled cup in his hands poured wine on the earth, and went about the pyre with endless moaning.

But at the hour when the morning star is a herald of light on the earth, the flames died down. The winds went back home again across the Thracian sea; and its waves roared under their feet. Then Achilles turned away from the burning pyre to rest, and sweet sleep sprang upon him. But Agamemnon and the others came again and at the noise he sat up awake again and said: "Agamemnon and you other chiefs of the Greek armies, first let us put out the burning pyre with wine, and then take up the bones of Patroclus, separating them well from the rest. Then let us place the bones in a golden urn with a double roll of fat around them till the time when I go myself down to Hades. But build no great mound till then. Later, you may build it high and wide, those of you who are left among the ships when I am gone."

And they did as he had said.

24

THEN each man went to his own ship, thinking of his supper and sweet sleep. But Achilles still thought, with tears, of his dead friend; and sleep, who overcomes all, could take no hold on him. He turned this way and that thinking of all they had done together and all they had gone through in the wars and on the unresting sea. And his tears ran as he lay now on his side, now on his back and now on his face; and he would get to his feet and walk up and down, half out of his mind, by the edge of the waves. And as Dawn came on the water he would take out his horses and chariot and drag Hector again. And when he had dragged him three times round

Patroclus' mound, he would rest in his hut again, but Hector he left outstretched on his face in the dust.

But the gods had pity for Hector and urged Hermes to take his body secretly away. This seemed good to all the rest but not to Hera or to Poseidon or to Athene, for Troy and Priam and his people were as hateful to them as ever, because of the sin of Paris; he had not taken their gifts but Aphrodite's when the goddesses came to his sheepfold. But on the twelfth morning Apollo said: "Hardhearted and cruel you gods are. Has Hector never burned thighs of bulls for you? Have you no heart to save him, dead though he is, for his wife and mother and child, and his father Priam and his people, who would burn him in the fire and give him his funeral? No, it is Achilles you would help, a man who is out of his mind, without pity or shame in his heart, shame which keeps men from wrong-doing and sometimes from better things, too. Let him take care that we do not become angry with him for this shameful handling of the dead."

Then Zeus sent Iris to bring Thetis. And Thetis put on a dark veil and went with Iris, and the sea waves opened before them. And they came to Heaven and found the far-voiced son of Cronos, and round him were sitting all the other gods that are forever. She sat down at the side of Zeus, where Athene gave up her place to her. Hera put a golden cup in her hand with words of comfort. And Thetis drank and gave back the cup. Then Zeus said: "You have come, Thetis, with great sorrow in your heart. I know it well. But let me tell you why I have sent for you. For nine days there has been division among the immortals over what Achilles, waster of cities, is doing with Hector's body. They are for having Hermes take the body away secretly, but I will do more honor than that to Achilles—to keep your love and respect in time to come. Go to your son now swiftly with my word. Tell him that the gods are angered with him, I more than all, for holding Hector at the ships. So he may fear me and give Hector back. And I will send Iris to great-hearted Priam to tell him to go to the Greek ships with gifts for Achilles which will make him glad."

And Thetis went from Olympus to her son's hut. She found him there moaning and round him the Myrmidons were getting their morning meal ready; they had killed a great woolly sheep. She sat down at his side and put her hand on his head and said: "My child, how long will you keep on eating your heart out with sorrow, with no thought either of food or rest? Good for you would be even a woman's arms. For you have not long now to live. Already death and the strong hand of fate are near you. But take good note of this, for I come from Zeus. He says that the gods are angered with you, and he more than all the immortals, because you hold Hector at the ships and have not given him back. Give him up now and take a ransom for the dead."

Then Achilles answered: "So be it. Let the ransom bringer take him away, if truly the Olympian so orders."

And Zeus sent Iris to Priam's house. She found it full of crying and moaning. His sons sat about their father in tears, and the old man's head and neck were covered with dirt which he had taken up from the earth in handfuls. His daughters and sons' wives were sorrowing throughout the house, thinking of all the Trojan fighters who had been killed by the Greeks. Iris came near to Priam and said: "Take courage, Priam, and fear not. I come to you from Zeus who, though far away, has care and pity for you. He orders you to give a ransom for Hector, taking gifts to Achilles to make his heart glad. You are to go by yourself with no other Trojan. A herald you may take, an old man to drive the mule wagon and bring back the dead man that Achilles killed. You are to have no thought or fear of death, for Zeus will send Hermes to bring you to Achilles. When you come to Achilles' hut, he will not kill you or let another do it, for he is not senseless or blind or wicked, and will respect one who comes with prayers."

Then the king told his sons to get the light-running mule wagon ready and put on it a basketwork box. And he himself went down into the high-roofed room, smelling of cedar wood, where he kept his treasures. And he told Hecuba his wife what he had to do, saying: "How does this seem to you? Tell me. As to myself, I desire strongly to go to the Greek ships."

But his wife cried aloud as she answered: "Alas! Where is the judgment you had in the eyes of strangers and your own people? How can you think of going by yourself to face the man who has killed so many of your sons? Your heart truly must be of iron. If he gets you in his power, he is so cruel and false, he will have no pity or respect for you."

The old man, godlike Priam, answered: "Do not attempt to keep me from going, or be a bird of ill-omen in my house.

You will not move me. If some mortal man had told me to go—some priest or seer—I might have thought it false. But I heard the voice of the goddess myself and saw her face to face. I will go and not let her words be for nothing. If it is my fate to lie dead at the Greek ships, so let it be. Let Achilles kill me, if I may take my son in my arms first and sorrow for him to the full."

He opened the chests and took out his gifts for Achilles: clothing and tripods and cauldrons and a very beautiful cup and ten talents of gold, so great was his desire to ransom his son. Then he drove the Trojans from the doorway with bitter words, crying: "Out with you, shame and dishonor to me that you are! Have you nothing to cry about at home, coming here to trouble me? Is it not enough that Zeus has sent me this sorrow, to have the best of my sons killed? You will find out about it quickly enough yourselves. Now that he is gone the Greeks will have no hard time killing you! As for me, may I go down into the house of Hades before I see the city wasted."

He drove them away with his stick and shouted with hard words to his sons. Helenus, Paris, Agathon, Pammon, Antiphonus, Polites, Deïphobus, Hippothoüs, and Dius; these nine he gave their orders: "Quick now, do-nothing children that are my shame! Would that you had all been killed in Hector's place! Unhappy that I am! I had the best sons in all Troy. Now, not one of them is left: not godlike Mestor, not Troïlus the brave charioteer, not Hector, that god among men; you would have thought he was an immortal's son. Ares has killed them all, and left me only these things of shame, false of tongue, light of heel, heroes of the dance, robbers of your own people's sheep. Will you not get me that wagon ready and put these things on it so that I may start?"

So he said, and in fear of their father's words, they brought the light-running wagon and while they were putting the mules to it and making Priam's own chariot ready, Hecuba came out to them, sad at heart, with a gold cup full of honey-hearted wine in her right hand. She stood before the horses and said: "Take this and pour your drink offering to Zeus, and pray that you may come back home safe, if you have made up your mind to go to the ships, whatever I say. Pray to the son of Cronos, Lord of the dark clouds, the god of Ida, who looks down over all Troy; pray for a bird of omen. If he will not send you one, then I certainly would not have you go however much you may want to."

And Priam answered: "Wife, I will not say 'No' to your request. It is good to lift up our hands to Zeus, to have pity on us if he may."

The old man made a woman servant pour water in a basin, and he washed his hands and took the cup from his wife and prayed, standing in the middle of the court, and made the drink offering with his eyes to Heaven, saying: "Father Zeus, you who rule from Ida, most glorious, most great, may I find welcome and pity under Achilles' roof; and, I pray you, send a bird of omen, dearest to you and greatest of birds; let him come on my right hand, so that seeing this sign I may, with that comfort, go my way to the Greek ships."

And Zeus the counselor heard him. He sent an eagle, the

most certain omen of all the birds that fly, the dark eagle which men name the black eagle, too. As wide as the door of some rich man's high-roofed treasure room his wings were and he came on the right, sailing over the city. When they saw him they were glad and all took heart.

Then the old man stepped quickly into his chariot and drove off through the echoing gateway. In front the mules pulled the four-wheeled wagon, driven by the herald, wise-hearted Idaeus, and the old man drove after him. His friends as they saw him off cried out as though he were going to his death. When they had gone down from the city to the plain, his sons and his daughters' husbands turned back, but Zeus, as he saw the two old men out on the plain, had pity and sent Hermes, his dear son, the Helper.

And Hermes, the killer of Argus, put on his beautiful sandals, immortal and golden, which carried him over sea and land as swift as the wind. And he took the rod with which he shuts men's eyes in sleep, or opens them when they are sleeping; and he came quickly to Troyland and the Helles-pont. He looked like a young prince at his fairest, with the beard first coming on his face.

Now when Priam and Idaeus had driven by the great mound of Ilus, they stopped at the river for the horses and mules to drink. Night had come down over the earth. The herald looked and saw Hermes near at hand, and he said to Priam: "We must think what to do now, Priam. I see a man getting ready to attack us. Let us fly in the chariot, or at least fall at his knees and pray for pity."

When he heard this, the old man was greatly afraid, his

hair stood on end and he did not know what to do. But the Helper came up and took him by the hand, saying: "Where are you going, father, with your horses and mules through the immortal night, when other men are sleeping? Are you not afraid of the cruel Greeks who are so near? If one of them saw you taking so much treasure through the swift black night, what would you do then? You are not young, yourself, and your friend here is too old to save you. Do not be afraid of me. I will even come to your defense, if need be, for you look to me like my own father."

Priam answered: "It is as you say, my dear son. But some god has stretched out his hand over me, sending someone so good-looking and wise-hearted as you to meet me. You must have very happy parents."

"That is true," said Hermes. "But, tell me truly, are you taking all these treasures to some ally to keep them for you safely, or are you all leaving Troy in fear, now that your son has fallen, who was the best man of you all, and never held back from the fighting?"

And Priam answered: "Who are you and who are your parents, my friend, to say such true things about my unhappy son? But come, tell me all. Is my son still by the ships, or has Achilles cut him to bits and thrown him to the dogs?"

And Hermes said: "Not yet, sir. I am Achilles' man and can tell you. He still lies by Achilles' ship as he was at first. This is the twelfth day, and though at Dawn every day Achilles drags him pitilessly round Patroclus' mound, you would wonder to see how clean and whole he is, and all his wounds are whole again. So well do the gods care for your son."

The old man's heart was glad to hear him and answered: "My child, see what a good thing it is to give the immortals their rightful offerings. My son Hector was never slow in this, and now the gods keep him in mind, dead though he is. But come, take this cup at my hands and, with Heaven's help, guide me to Achilles' hut."

Then Hermes said: "You are testing me, sir, offering me gifts of which Achilles knows nothing. I have too much fear and respect for him to take anything without his knowledge. But I will be your guide gladly."

So saying, the Helper sprang onto the chariot behind the horses and took the whip and reins. They came to the ditch and wall which guarded the ships as the watchers were getting their supper ready. And Hermes sent them all to sleep and opened the gates and brought Priam and his wagon of treasures through. Then they came to the high-roofed hut which the Myrmidons had built for their king. They had roofed it with grass and put round it a wide court walled in with thick stakes. The gate to it was held by one great bar of fir. This took three of the Greeks to put it in place, three of the other Greeks, but Achilles would drive it home by himself. Hermes opened this for the old man and brought in his glorious gifts for Achilles; then he stepped down from the chariot and said: "Sir, it is I, immortal Hermes, who came with you, for my father sent me. Now I will go back and not be seen by Achilles. But go in to the son of Peleus, take his knees in your hands, and pray him by his father and his fair-haired mother and his child; so you may move him."

Then Hermes went back to high Olympus. But Priam left Idaeus to hold the horses and mules and went straight to Achilles' house. There he found Achilles—with two of the Myrmidons, Automedon and Alcimus, waiting upon him. Achilles had made an end of eating and drinking; the table still stood by his side. Priam came in without being seen and went and took Achilles' knees in his hands and kissed Achilles' hands—the terrible hands which had killed so many of his sons. And Achilles wondered as he saw him and the others wondered and looked one at another. Then Priam said in prayer: "Think of your father, O godlike Achilles, of your father who is even as I am, at the sad doorway of old age. It may be that those who live near him trouble him and that he has no one to keep war and destruction from him. Still, when he hears that you are living, he is happy and hopes day after day to see his dear son come back from Troyland. But I—unhappy I am. My sons were the bravest in all Troy and now not one of them is alive. And the last of them and the bravest, Hector, that by himself guarded Troy and her people, you killed but now, as he fought for his country. So I have come to the Greek ships to win his body back with a ransom too great to be counted. Achilles, fear the anger of Heaven, think of your own father and take pity on me. I am more to be pitied even than he is, for I have made myself do what no other man has done, and have stretched out my hand to the face of him who killed my sons."

So Priam said; and in Achilles he awakened a desire to sorrow aloud for his father; and he took the old man's hands and gently put him from him. And the two sorrowed bitterly—Priam, at Achilles' feet, for man-killing Hector and Achilles for his own father, and now again for Patroclus, and the sound of their moaning went up through the house.

But when Achilles had had enough of sorrowing, and the desire for it had gone from his heart and body, he sprang from his seat and lifted up the old man by the hand, pitying his white head and snowy beard. Then he said: "Ah, unhappy man, many are your sorrows truly. How did you have the heart to come by yourself to the Greek ships to meet my eyes? I have killed many of your brave sons. Your heart truly must be of iron. But come, be seated, and we will let our sorrows be quiet in our hearts, whatever our pain, for moaning will not help us. The gods have spun the thread for us this way—to live in pain, all we who die—but they themselves are without sorrow. Two urns stand on the floor of Zeus and in one are good gifts and in the other evil. And the man for whom Zeus, Lord of the thunder, mixes the gifts he sends, that man will meet now with evil, now with good; but the man to whom he gives only his evil gifts must journey over the face of the sacred earth unhonored either by gods or men. To my father Peleus the gods were good from his birth; for they made him king over the Myrmidons and though he was but a man they gave him a goddess to be his wife. But even to him they sent evil, for they gave him an only son fated to die young. And now I cannot take any care of him as he grows old, but must stay here in Troyland, far from my own country, troubling you and your children. And you, too, Priam, we hear, were happy in times past, but in the end Heaven sent this evil upon you, that war and death are ever about your city. But give the pain in your heart some rest. Sorrowing for your son will not make him live again. Before that some other evil will come upon you."

Then Priam answered: "Say not to me, Achilles, 'Be seated,' while Hector lies uncared for among the huts. Give him back to me quickly and let me look upon him; and do you take the great ransom we bring. So may you go back safely to your own country and be happy there—because you have let me live and see the light of the sun."

But with eyes of flame swift-footed Achilles answered: "Anger me no more, old man. I am minded myself to give Hector back to you, for from Zeus the word came to me by my mother Thetis, daughter of the old man of the sea. And well do I know, Priam, that it was not without the help of the gods that you came here. No mortal man, however young and strong, would be brave enough; or be able to push back the bar of our gate. So move my heart no more, or I may still sin against the will of Zeus and not even here under my roof will you be safe, for all your prayers."

And the old man was afraid and seated himself. But Achilles, like a lion, sprang through the door of the house, and with him went Automedon and Alcimus, nearest of all to his heart now that Patroclus was dead. And they loosed the horses from Priam's car and took Idaeus in and gave him a seat. They lifted the ransom down from the wagon. But they left a fair shirt and two covers there so that Achilles could fold the body in them when he sent it back to Troy. And Achilles made the women take Hector's body aside and wash and put oil on it, keeping it out of Priam's view. For Priam on seeing it might cry out in his bitter sorrow and not keep his anger in, and Achilles himself then might be moved to anger and kill him and sin against the will of Zeus. And when the women had washed and put oil upon it and clothed it, Achilles himself with his men lifted the body upon the polished wagon. As he did so he moaned and cried to his dead friend by name: "O Patroclus! Be not angry with me, if even in the house of Hades you hear that I have given Hector back to his dear father. Great enough are the gifts and they are yours as well as mine."

So he cried and then went back into the house and seated himself over against Priam and said: "Your son, old sir, I have given back to you and you may see him at dawn, as you take him with you. But now, let us think of supper. For even fair-haired Niobe took food at last, though her twelve children had been killed in her house; her six sons by Apollo, with arrows from his silver bow, and her six daughters by Artemis the Archer. This was because Niobe matched herself against Leto saying that the goddess had two children only; so those two children put to death all Niobe's twelve. For nine days they lay before her in their blood, for Zeus made all the people like stones. But on the tenth day the gods gave them a funeral and then Niobe thought of food, tired out as she was with weeping. Somewhere now, high up in the lonely mountains among the rocks where, they say, the nymphs sleep, there, though turned to a stone, she still thinks

of what the gods did. So now too, father, let us take food.
You may weep over your dear son later, as much as you will,
in Troy."

And he sprang up and killed a white sheep and his men
skinned it and made it ready and cut it up and put it over
the fire. And there was bread in fair baskets on the table
and Achilles served the meat. And when they had put
from them the desire of food and drink, then Priam looked
at and wondered at Achilles, seeing how beautiful and tall
he was, for he was like the gods to look on. And Achilles
looked at and wondered at Priam, noting his kingly air
and words. And when they had looked at one another so,
Priam said: "Take me now to my bed, O King, so that sweet
sleep may give us rest. My eyes have not been shut from the
day on which your hands took my son's life. Now, at last,
I have tasted food and drunk wine; before this, nothing."

And Achilles gave orders to put beds under the front
part of the roof, with fair purple coverings of wool; and the
women with lights in their hands quickly made the beds
ready. And Achilles said to Priam: "Dear sir, rest here, but
take care that no chief of the Greeks sees you. If one of them
saw you in the swift black night, he might tell Agamemnon,
and then we might have to wait before giving back the
dead. How many days do you need for Hector's funeral?
For how long must I keep back the Greeks?"

And the old man, godlike Priam, answered: "You know
how narrowly we are shut within the city; and how far off
the wood on the mountain is—and the Trojans are much
afraid. Give us nine days in which to sorrow over Hector;

on the tenth we will give him his funeral and let the people feast. On the eleventh we will build the mound over him and on the twelfth, fight again, if we must."

And Achilles said: "All this, old Priam, will be as you have said. I will hold back the battle for as long as you want." So saying, he took the old man's right hand in his, to keep him from any fear, and they went to their rest. Priam and the herald lay in the front part of the house with wise thoughts in their hearts, but Achilles in the innermost room, with fair-faced Briseis at his side.

Now all the other gods and men slept the night long, but sleep could not take hold of Hermes, the Helper, as he thought how he could guide Priam back unnoted by the watch guard at the gate. He stood at the king's head, saying: "Have you no thought of evil, sir, sleeping so among the Greeks, because Achilles did not kill you? You have ransomed your son, it is true, and a great price you gave. But if Agamemnon hears of you, your sons will have to give three times as much for your ransom."

At that the king was much afraid and made the herald get up. And Hermes put the mules and horses to and drove them out of the camp without anyone knowing.

But when they came to the ford of eddying Xanthus, offspring of immortal Zeus, Hermes went back to high Olympus, and Dawn was coming over the face of all the earth. And they drove to the city with many moans and cries, and on the wagon was the dead. No one was conscious of their coming, but only Cassandra, high up on Pergamus, saw her dear father standing in his chariot, and that other lying on the bier in the mule wagon. At that, she cried out loudly over the town: "Come, men and women of Troy, and look upon Hector, if ever in his life you were joyful to see him come back from battle, for great joy he was to the city and all the people."

So she cried, and every man and woman in the city came out to meet Priam as he brought home the dead. First Hector's dear wife and queenly mother threw themselves upon the wagon, holding his head, and the people crowded about them sorrowing. And all day long they would have sorrowed there in tears for Hector, if the old king had not shouted from the chariot: "Make way for the mules to go through. Later, you may have all you will of sorrowing, when I have brought him to his house."

Then they made room for the wagon. When they had brought him into the glorious house, they placed him on a corded bed and stationed singers by his side, who sang over him as was his right while the women joined in with the sorrowing. And among them white-armed Andromache, holding man-killing Hector's head in her hands, sang: "Husband, gone from life you are, still young, leaving me a widow in your house. Your son is still a child, the son born to you and to me, ill-fated as we were. I do not think he will come to be a man. Before that this city will be no more. For you watched over and guarded it, keeping its wives and little children safe. But now you are dead. Before long, now, all these will be sailing away in the hollow ships and I among them. You, my child, will be put to work under some cruel master. Or, maybe, some Greek will throw you from our

walls—for some brother or son or father that Hector killed. Many have bitten the great earth at his hands, for in battle he was not gentle. Therefore the people sorrow for him throughout the city. More than all thought is the sorrow you have left to your parents, Hector, and to me still more, for you did not stretch out your arms to me as you lay dying or say words I might have lived with night and day."

And Hecuba in turn sorrowed: "Hector, dearest to my heart of all my children, the gods loved you in your life and when you were dead they had care of you. When Achilles took my other sons, he would sometimes sell them oversea, to Samnos and Imbros and Lemnos where the smoke goes up. But when he killed you he dragged you round Patroclus' mound, though that would not bring Patroclus to life. But now you lie here untouched as if you had but now died from Apollo's gentle arrow."

And Helen, third, took up the cry of sorrow: "Hector, dearest of my husband's brothers! Would I had died before Paris brought me here! In all these years never have I heard a hard or ungentle word from you. If anyone, a brother of yours, or sister, or brother's wife, or your mother, was unkind—but your father was as kind as if he had been my own—you would stop them and soften them with your goodwill and gentle words. Therefore I sorrow both for you and for myself. I have no longer in all Troy anyone that is kind and gentle to me; but all men turn from me as they go by."

And the great crowd joined with her in her sorrow. Then Priam said: "Bring wood now into the city. And do not be

afraid of an ambush. Achilles, when he sent me back from the ships, gave me his word that they will not attack before the twelfth dawn comes."

Then they put oxen and mules to their wagons and for nine days brought in great quantities of wood, but when the tenth dawn came, giving light to men, they took dead Hector, with many tears, and put him on the top of the pyre, and threw fire on it. Then, when early Dawn, the rose-fingered, came on the eleventh day, the people crowded together again about Hector's pyre. They put out the fire with wine, and his brothers and friends took up the white bones, sorrowing and in tears. They placed them in a golden urn, covering them over with soft purple cloth, and quickly put the urn in a hollow grave and covered it with great well-ordered stones. Then swiftly they built up the mound, with men on the lookout on all sides, against an attack by the Greeks before the time. When they had built the mound they went back and honored him with a glorious feast in the house of Priam, Zeus-cared-for king.

Such was the funeral of Hector, tamer of horses.